ABOUT THE AUTHOR

CHRISTOPHER REEVE has established a reputation as one of the country's leading actors, and since he was paralyzed in an equestrian competition in 1995, he has put a human face on spinal cord injury. Reeve is the chairman of the board of the Christopher Reeve Paralysis Foundation (CRPF) and vice chairman of the National Organization on Disability, and he lobbies vigorously for health-care reform and funding for research. He is the author of the bestselling book *Still Me* and lives in upstate New York with his wife, Dana, and their children.

ABOUT THE PHOTOGRAPHER

MATTHEW REEVE is a recent graduate of Brown University with a B.A. in art semiotics. He has previously worked for ABC News and MTV Europe. He is currently a freelance photographer and independent filmmaker whose first full-length documentary was distributed worldwide in 2003. Matthew divides his time between London and New York.

Also by Christopher Reeve

Still Me

Nothing Is Impossible

Reflections on a New Life

Christopher Reeve

WITH IMAGES

BY MATTHEW REEVE

arrow books

Published by Arrow Books in 2003

1 3 5 7 9 10 8 6 4 2

Copyright © Cambria Productions, Inc. 2002

Christopher Reeve has asserted his right under the Copyright, Designs
and Patents Act, 1988 to be identified as the author of this work

First published in the United Kingdom in 2002 by Century

Arrow Books Limited
The Random House Group Limited
20 Vauxhall Bridge Road, London SW1V 2SA

Random House Australia (Pty) Limited
20 Alfred Street, Milsons Point, Sydney,
New South Wales 2061, Australia

Random House New Zealand Limited
18 Poland Road, Glenfield, Auckland 10, New Zealand

Random House (Pty) Limited
Endulini, 5a Jubilee Road, Parktown 2193, South Africa

The Random House Group Limited Reg. No. 954009
www.randomhouse.co.uk

A CIP catalogue record for this book is available from the
British Library

Papers used by Random House are natural, recyclable products
made from wood grown in sustainable forests.
The manufacturing processes conform to the environmental
regulations of the country of origin

ISBN 0 09 944659 6

Printed and bound in the United Kingdom by
Cox & Wyman Ltd, Reading, Berkshire

For Dana, Matthew,
Alexandra, and Will,
without whom nothing
would be possible

Acknowledgments

Ann Godoff, at Random House, did me the great honor of approving this book without delay and editing it herself. Sunshine Lucas was an excellent liaison between us, answering questions tirelessly and—befitting her name—cheerfully throughout the process. Jennifer Walsh, my literary agent at William Morris, represented both the book and me personally with the utmost integrity and professionalism.

The original idea was to compile excerpts from speeches and interviews I'd given from 1995 through 2002. I want to thank Sarah Houghton, Diana De Rosa, Maggie Goldberg, and Shyrlee Greenberg for the countless hours they spent transcribing my spoken words and their gracious acceptance of the fact that I found 99 percent of them unusable. Now I know that improvised remarks don't always translate well onto the written page.

I want to thank Rachel Strife, Karen Gerwin, Liza Cohen, and especially June Fox and my assistant, Laurie Hawkins, for all the time they spent sitting next to me at the computer, patiently waiting for the next sentence. I'm also grateful for their invaluable comments and suggestions as we proceeded.

I'll be forever grateful to Therapeutic Alliances, Inc., for the ERGYS 2 bicycle; to Pulmonetic Systems, Inc., for the LTV Pressure Support Ventilator; to Nellcor for the Pulse Oximeter and computerized carbon dioxide meter; and to Bioflex, Inc., for the FES Stim Machine. That equipment has kept me (and I hope will keep others) in good health and out of the hospital.

My nurses and aides work incredibly long hours and have honored our whole family with their skill and commitment. I would especially like to mention Dolly Arro, Eileen Adams, Bill Bernhey, Sue Citarella, Maggie Choa, Henry Ryan, Marlou Sanchez, Shelley Griesinger, Patrick Connors, Chris Fantini, Rob Clarke, Jim Hartigan, Greg Coyle, Mark Pawelec, Frank Palmer, and Mike Ricci.

Dr. Harlan Weinberg and Dr. Steven Kirshblum have gone way beyond the call of duty to help and advise me since my return home. The X-ray and ultrasound technicians at Northern Westchester Hospital are terrific; however, I hope to see them less frequently in the future. The same goes for Doctors Howard Levin, Oren Kahn,

Steven Bernstein, David Bank, Eric Johnson, and Eli Abe-meyer, who have all helped to keep me in one piece. Dr. John McDonald and his associates at Washington University pushed me to the limit in conducting their study. Dr. Linda Schultz, his indefatigable assistant, deserves tremendous credit for making it happen.

I want to thank everyone at the Christopher Reeve Paralysis Foundation and the Christopher and Dana Reeve Paralysis Resource Center, all of whom continually renew their dedication and efforts to help people living with paralysis. My publicist, Wes Combs, has done an outstanding job of communicating our message to the public. Special thanks go to Michael Manganiello, director of government affairs at CRPF, for his extraordinary loyalty to me and his fierce dedication to the cause.

Finally, I want to thank my extended family—all the Reeves, Johnsons, Pitneys, and Morosinis. Above all, I want to say thank you to my wife, Dana, who is also my best friend and most helpful critic. There is not enough room on the page for me to list all the unique characteristics and accomplishments of Matthew, Alexandra, and Will. I hope this book will give you some idea of how much they mean to me.

Contents

Nothing Is Impossible

The First Decision

As the old saying goes, you better know what
you want because you might get it and you've
got to accept it. Whether you succeed or
whether you encounter adversity, you always
have to believe in your worth as a person.
That's what counts.

—*Remarks at a success seminar in
Portland, Oregon, February 6, 2001*

When I made those comments in 2001, it was no longer difficult for me to say to anyone that you have to believe in your worth as a person. But in the intensive care unit at the University of Virginia on June 1, 1995, I had no such belief. Far from it. On that day I regained consciousness to find myself lying in traction, a heavy metal ball suspended behind my head attached to a metal frame secured by screws in each temple. I learned that as the result of a fall during an equestrian competition I had broken my neck just centimeters below the brain stem, and that my chances of surviving the surgery to reattach my head to my spinal column were 50/50 at best. Even if the operation was successful, I would still remain paralyzed from the shoulders down and unable to breathe on my own. I heard the whooshing sound of a ventilator as it pumped oxygen into my lungs through a long tube inserted into a hole in my neck. I've lived with that sound for many years.

The moment I understood the gravity of my situation my immediate reaction was that such a life was unacceptable, even though I knew absolutely nothing about living as a vent-dependent quadriplegic. I realized that there was no cure for spinal cord injuries like mine and that I would forever be dependent on others for the basic necessities of daily existence. My role as a husband and the father of three children would be severely compromised, because paralysis had suddenly transformed me into a forty-two-year-old infant. I thought it would be selfish and unfair to remain alive.

I remember going over my life, taking an inventory of all the cuts, bruises, broken bones, and illnesses I had weathered, ranging from mononucleosis to malaria and mastocytosis (a rare disease that destroys red blood cells as they emerge from the bone marrow). At age sixteen, I developed alopecia areata, a condition that causes patches of baldness in an otherwise healthy head of hair. Fortunately I was able to comb over the spots, and there were long periods of remission when the baldness disappeared. I was a survivor; I always had been. A part of me insisted that this situation shouldn't be any different; another part acknowledged that this time I had gone over the edge and was free-falling into the unknown.

The month I spent in the intensive care unit was an emotional roller-coaster ride created by my own inner turmoil and contradictions coming from those involved in my case. The critical care was nothing short of miraculous. Dr. John Jane—arguably one of the best neurosurgeons in the world—achieved the nearly impossible feat of reattaching the base of my skull to my spinal column with wire, titanium, and bone grafted from my hip. Under his watchful eye, a team of internists and pulmonologists cured me of ulcers and pneumonia. By the second week I was able to turn my head about half an inch from side to side, and I could raise my shoulders slightly. Dr. Jane was confident that before too long I would be able to move my deltoids, which might lead to the functional recovery of my right arm. Perhaps I could learn to feed myself, and someday be able to drive a specially adapted car. My spirits rose.

In the third week of June I was visited by Dr. Marcalee Sipski, director of the Spinal Cord Injury Unit at the Kessler Rehabilitation Institute in West Orange, New Jersey. My wife, Dana, and my younger brother, Benjamin, had surveyed rehab centers from Georgia to Colorado and concluded that Kessler was the best choice, because I would receive the highest quality care without having to go far from home. Dr. Sipski gave me a thorough examination and then told me point blank that my injury was "complete"—meaning that the cord had been severed at the second cervical vertebra (known as "C–2"). Signals from the brain would never be able to get past the injury site. Without any direction from above, the spinal cord would remain useless and the skin, muscles, bones, and tissues of my body would begin a steady progression of atrophy and decay. All I knew about the regeneration of cut or damaged nerves was that it was possible in the peripheral nervous system but not in the central nervous system.

I asked questions about the spinal cord and why the nerves inside it could not regenerate. Usually I had these conversations late at night with the residents and nurses on duty in the unit. (The days were filled with family, visitors, and the routines of necessary care.) Nobody claimed to know for certain, but the prevailing explanation was that it had to do with evolution. An animal paralyzed by a spinal cord injury would most likely be a ready–to–serve meal for another animal higher on the food chain. Even if nerve regeneration in the spinal cord was possible it couldn't happen quickly, so the injured animal would still be easy prey. Without medical intervention the victim of a spinal cord injury— animal or human—usually dies within hours or days, depending on the severity of the case. Almost every one of these late–night discussions ended with the conclusion that I should just consider myself lucky to be alive. I wasn't so sure.

Apparently no one in my little nighttime universe knew that a handful of scientists around the world had been investigating the possibility of regeneration in the spinal cord as early as the 1970s. In 1981 Dr. Alberto Aguayo, at McGill University in Montreal, using a cocktail of growth-enhancing chemicals, achieved regeneration and modest functional recovery in rats.

I only began to focus on spinal cord research in early September 1995. Until then my primary concern was survival, not only for me as a patient but for Dana and my three children, Matthew (fifteen), Alexandra (eleven), and Will (three). Their love and the love that flowed from my extended family, as well as from friends and even complete strangers all over the world, had saved me from my initial desire to end it all. In 2002, seven years after the accident and in the year of my fiftieth birthday, I look back with almost indescribable gratitude at the moment when Dana knelt by my bedside and said, "You're still you, and I love you."

Her simple but profound declaration became the basis for my autobiography, *Still Me*, which was published in 1998. But in describing that scene I never mentioned one critical detail: in response to my thoughts about ending my life, she said that we should wait for at least two years. Then, if I still felt the same, we could find a way to let me go. On one level, you could say she used the oldest selling technique in the book: you offer customers a free trial, a free sample, with no obligation and no money down, in order to get them on the hook. On another level, a much deeper one where our love and respect for each other has always lived, she knew that I was only in the first stage of a natural reaction to tragedy. Asking me to wait was the perfect course of action. She was giving me room, the freedom to make a choice, yet knowing what that choice would be in time.

The first decision flowed from Dana's words and the look on the faces of all three children when they came into my room. While Dana supported the option to reconsider the value of life at a point in the future, I could tell in an instant that the children wanted me to live and be there for them *now*. I consented to the surgery. I gave the doctors permission to suction secretions out of my lungs and use IV antibiotics to treat the pneumonia that otherwise would have caused my death. Although I didn't realize it at the time, I had chosen the path toward survival. Inner turmoil and the highs and lows caused by contradictory information would become the norm, but there would be no turning back.

First I had to learn to swallow. Even though I passed

the test, the smell and taste of food were repulsive. A feeding tube was inserted into my stomach, and during the night a bagful of mocha-colored goop containing essential nutrients dripped down a long catheter into the site. Once a day a team of nurses and physical therapists transferred me into a wheelchair and pushed me down a corridor into the dayroom, where I could receive visitors and have someone in my family read letters to me for no more than thirty minutes. Then it was back to bed.

I couldn't believe how complicated this daily excursion was. First my head and neck had to be immobilized in a rigid cervical collar. Then Ace bandages were wrapped around most of my torso in order to keep my blood pressure from dropping when I sat up. Next a rigid sheet of plastic called a sliding board was positioned under my body; two nurses rolled me onto my side while two others slid the board into place. Before the transfer into the wheelchair I was gradually pushed up into a sitting position on the bed. My blood pressure was monitored every ninety seconds. Sometimes I would faint, which meant a ten- to fifteen-minute wait before another attempt. On a bad day it might take two or three tries. On a good day I could achieve sitting up with a stabilized blood pressure in about twenty minutes. When I could sit up without "crashing" we were ready for the big maneuver. The wheelchair was placed against the left side of the bed and its right arm removed. The bed was lowered to the level of the wheelchair. I lay flat again and my team of helpers carefully dragged the sliding board over to form a bridge between the wheelchair and the bed. The next step was sitting up again. If that was successful, I was gently placed in the chair and the board was taken away. After a few minutes of adjusting to being in the wheelchair, I was pushed down the corridor and into the dayroom.

As I started to face reality during the month in intensive care and six months in rehab, moments from my former life kept popping into my head. It was like a slide show, but the pictures were all out of sequence, as if they had been placed randomly in the projector. As a long plastic tube was inserted through my neck and pushed down into my lungs to remove accumulating fluid, suddenly I would be sailing in Maine. But before the next slide appeared on the screen in my mind, secretions were being suctioned up the tube. A moment or two later, Dana and I were making love; I was on a horse jumping over stone walls in the countryside; I was taking a curtain call after a performance in the theater, carrying boxes and lugging furniture up four flights of stairs into my first apartment in New York. Then it was four in the morning, and two aides had woken me up by turning me over onto my other side so that my skin wouldn't break down from lying in one position too long. Even though I was flipped from side to side every two hours at night for nearly three years after my injury, I almost never slept through it. More images flashed on the screen, usually snapshots of my most cherished memories when I was whole and healthy and free.

Psychologists came to the bedside, but their tone was often patronizing and I was usually relieved when they went away. I had to read the *Spinal Cord Manual*, which had little to say about patients with my level of injury. I had to choose a color for my new Sip–N–Puff wheelchair, which would allow me to drive by myself without being pushed. I had to locate a specially equipped accessible van with four-wheel drive, heavy-duty shock absorbers, and a mechanical lift. I had to approve plans for remodeling our house so that I could work, eat, and sleep all on one floor. There were dozens of other issues that had to be faced. Reality was now my new identity as a C–2 vent–dependent quadriplegic. My vision for the future prior to three o'clock on May 27, 1995, I now classified as what would have been a normal life. Everything after that instant I now had to accept as the new reality. Deep inside I was angry, and I probably still carry much of that anger with me today.

But the critical factor was that in spite of myself, I was adjusting to my new life.

Dana's intuition about what my state of mind would be two years after the accident proved to be absolutely right: I was glad to be alive, not out of obligation to others, but because life was worth living. By May 27, 1997, we were settled in our bedroom in the new wing of our home north of New York City, having camped out in the dining room for more than six months. *In the Gloaming,* a film I directed for HBO, had premiered in late April and been warmly received by the critics and the public. I had become the spokesman for HealthExtras, a company based in Maryland that offers low-cost supplemental insurance to cover nonmedical expenses in the event of a catastrophic illness or disability. The American Paralysis Association, founded by Henry Stifel, Sr., in 1982 after his son Henry suffered a spinal cord injury at age seventeen, had now become the Christopher Reeve Paralysis Foundation. Although it was still run by a small staff in a Springfield, New Jersey, office building, the annual research budget had grown from $300,000 to more than $3 million. I was healthy enough to accept speaking engagements around the country, even though the travel required private planes, three nurses, two aides, and a coordinator of logistics and accessibility.

Today I am probably busier than I was before the accident. I have to juggle physical therapy, my responsibilities at the foundation and as vice-chairman of the National Organization on Disability, writing, producing, directing, family, friends, travel, and much more. When people ask if I am disturbed by the fact that others pity me, I have to admit that the problem actually is that everyone seems to assume I can do almost anything.

On a Thursday in late April 2002, Dana and I received an invitation from the king of Spain to fly to Barcelona for the weekend. The offer was to attend a Formula One race with the royal family that Saturday afternoon, followed by a small private dinner and an appearance at a party around midnight. On Sunday we were to have lunch at a nearby seaside resort before returning to New York that evening on the king's private jet. Needless to say we would have been there in a heartbeat, except for a few details. When our logistics coordinator, Diana De Rosa, contacted all the king's men (or at least those involved in planning the weekend), she gave them the dimensions of my wheelchair and soon discovered that there was room for me at the racetrack, but not at the party. Apparently our attendance at that occasion was very important to the king, but no entrance to the venue was at least thirty-one inches wide. Diana never got around to listing some of the other requirements for the trip: a hospital bed with an inflatable mattress, supplemental oxygen, voltage converters for the ventilator and the battery charger for the wheelchair, accommodations for an entourage of at least seven or eight people, and contingency plans with a first-rate hospital in case of an emergency.

Whenever I travel, all those issues have to be taken into consideration, but nine times out of ten I go. In 1995, a trip down the corridor to a hospital dayroom was an arduous journey. In 2002, a weekend trip to Spain was only a question of relatively minor logistics. Unfortunately the invitation was politely withdrawn.

ON MAY 3, 2002, DANA AND I HOSTED THE RIBBON-cutting ceremony for the CRPF's new Paralysis Resource Center near our main office in Springfield. Funded by the government through the Centers for Disease Control in Atlanta, it is *the* source of information for anyone newly paralyzed or living with paralysis for any reason. Simply by going to www.paralysis.org on the Internet, patients and their caregivers can access our website and find referrals to accessibility, assisted living, transportation, job opportunities, recreation, and much more. Sometimes it seems that Dana and I were looking for answers to many of those questions just the other day.

Suddenly seven years have gone by and we're in a position to give advice. What I say to others depends on
their condition. I tell people who have been injured recently and are still contemplating suicide that life is
worth living. Many respond well to the fact that there
are no absolutes. I try to lift their spirits by making light
of some research. Scientists reverse their findings all the
time: first they say coffee is okay, and then they say it's
not. They go back and forth about the benefits of red
wine, butter versus margarine, how long a mother
should breast-feed, and how many times a week (if any)
you should eat eggs. What about all the people who are
up and around long after a doctor told them they had
only six months to live or would never walk again?
Some people live with paralysis but don't take care of
their health. I suggest that they eat properly and try to
find a way to exercise. It might help with recovery; at
the very least it will mean fewer visits to the hospital.

Occasionally I hear from people with spinal cord
injuries who have been sitting in a wheelchair for as
much as twenty-one years. Some tell me that there is no
point in searching for a cure; others even say they are
happy with life the way it is and don't want to be cured.
It's difficult for me to understand their point of view,
but I completely respect those individuals as long as
they don't try to interfere with progress. Less than a

generation ago it would have been almost irrelevant to ask a patient with Parkinson's, Alzheimer's, diabetes, muscular dystrophy, ALS, or a spinal cord injury not to stand in the way of progress, simply because there wasn't much. Today all that has changed. Since the time of my injury, scientists all over the world have been steadily moving forward, although they are not progressing as rapidly as many patients would like. At least they have been saying publicly, and most of us believe privately, that it is no longer appropriate or necessary to use the word "impossible."

Humor

TEACHER:

"Why weren't you in class yesterday?"

STUDENT:

"Sir, I wasn't feeling very well."

TEACHER:

"The only excuse for nonattendance is
quadruple amputation. But even then,
they can still bring you to class
in a basket."

—*My twelfth-grade English teacher,*
George Packard, and a classmate,
Princeton Day School, 1970

When things are really bad, you have to laugh. We use humor to relieve tension and cope with many things in life that are whimsical and even absurd. Humor can camouflage jealousy, prejudice, and intolerance. It can bring people together by common reference, which was one of the reasons I enjoyed being an actor. My injury gave me firsthand knowledge that humor is also one of the best ways—if not *the* best way—to channel anger.

Visitors to my bedside at UVA later remarked that I appeared calm and even surprisingly peaceful so soon after a major catastrophe. Inside, though, I was angry down to my very core. I remember trying my hardest to seem relaxed for the sake of certain family members, particularly Will. He understood that I had broken my neck and couldn't move, but he didn't know much about the future. Dana and I wanted more than any-thing to keep him from becoming traumatized by the situation. While I drifted in and out of consciousness, she played with him in the dayroom and was able to make him understand that I was the same Dad, but dif-ferent.

Although we managed to spare Will from seeing the dark side of his injured father, my younger brother, Ben, my mother, Barbara, and Dana had to bear the brunt of my outrage. They knew all too well that one of the worst traits of my personality is perfectionism. A particularly bad example for them must have been a visit just before the first press conference after my surgery. I made it clear—actually I repeatedly *demanded*—that they must convince the media and everyone else that I was an experienced, capable rider fully qualified to compete in a cross-country jumping event. I was in-jured in a freak accident, not a foolish one.

Fortunately, in the midst of my efforts to get the word out from my point of view, which for me was no laughing matter, others began to see the lighter side. Not unexpectedly, first out of the box was *Saturday Night Live*, which reported the following news item on their "Weekend Update":

"Christopher Reeve says that the humor of Robin

Williams gave him the will to live. The humor of Pauly Shore, however, makes him long for the sweet release of death."

Next out was Howard Stern:

"Too bad about Christopher Reeve. But man, his wife is a *babe*."

Then a sick joke started to circulate around the country, which made its way back to me in June of '95:

"Q: What's the difference between Christopher Reeve and O. J. Simpson?

A: "O. J. walks."

Looking back now, I'm grateful to the media and the public for breaking the ice, for introducing humor at a time when there was ongoing daily coverage about the gravity of my situation. I had just learned to tolerate partially deflating the trachea tube (the "trache") inside my neck. That allowed air to pass over my vocal cords, so I could speak instead of just mouthing words. It was a big step forward, both practically and psychologically: for the first three or four weeks I wanted all the air to go directly into my lungs.

Now that I could talk and had become fair game for comedy, I was ready to try some of my own:

Nurse, arriving in the morning: "How are you today?"

Me: "Well, my throat's a little scratchy, I have an itch on my nose, and my fingernails need cutting. Oh—and I'm paralyzed."

I remember thoroughly embarrassing another nurse her first day on the job. I had been treated for a skin breakdown in the sacral area, which had plagued me for months but finally healed. Lying on my left side I asked her, "How's my butt?" She replied, "It looks great to me." I said, "I know *that*. But what about my skin?" She turned crimson. For a moment I thought I'd lost her, but thankfully she came back for her next shift, and after all these years she's still here checking out my butt on a daily basis.

I'm happy to say that most of the seventeen nurses and aides who work with me today have been part of the team since I came home in December of '95. Over time they have transformed from "health care professionals" to extended family. Many of them were initially intimidated by me, so I tried to use humor to make the new recruits more comfortable. Most of my efforts were rather pathetic, but they were still necessary to ease frustration and manage anger. Sometimes I would pull up to a door and then bark to be let out. During the morning ritual of putting new bandages on my neck at the trache site, a nurse would ask if the seal was tight enough. If I was happy with it, I would bark like a seal.

Once a nurse asked me if I liked my wheelchair. I told her I didn't exactly *like* it but it was a good thing to legally drink and drive at the same time.

Jokes about the wheelchair helped defuse my anger about being in one. I also quickly discovered that when I appeared in public it was best to begin with a light remark to put the audience at ease. At the Oscars in March 1996, my opening line was, "What you probably don't know is that I left New York last September and I just got here today. But I'm glad I did, because I wouldn't have missed this welcome for anything in the world." Knowing that Jay Leno is an avid car collector, I made him an offer on *The Tonight Show*: "When I'm out of this chair you can take it, put a Chevy 350 engine in it, and blast down the freeway." When David Letterman asked me how I was doing, I told him and the audience, "I was fine, but I think I broke my neck again driving over all the potholes on my way into the city."

In the process of adjusting to my new life, I began to enjoy slightly sick or inappropriate humor the most. Of all the performances in the 1997 ABC special *Christopher Reeve: A Celebration of Hope*, I particularly appreciated that of Chris Fonseca, a Mexican comedian with cerebral palsy. He complained about the woman who received a $2.9 million settlement from McDonald's after spilling scalding-hot coffee in her lap, saying, "I've done that. But I kinda liked it. Do I owe *them* money?" Then he told us, "I was in a restaurant awhile back. I started choking. I tried to get help. [He made frantic gestures with his hands.] Wouldn't you know it, I accidentally proposed to a deaf girl! So I'm married now."

When I was in rehab, my friend Treat Williams came to visit and found me in the dayroom. His first words: "Don't get up." Another friend described a sailing trip with a crew made up of a guy with only one leg, another who had a heart condition, and a third man with a broken arm who could only work the starboard side of the boat. My response: "You should have invited me. I would have fit right in."

Recently a leading neuroscientist told me that brain damage can help the injured spinal cord recover. Apparently motor neurons can regenerate fairly easily in the brain and then migrate down into the cord. I guess the logical conclusion is that if you are going to end up paralyzed, you might as well smash your head at the same time. Then there would be good news and bad news: you would walk out of the hospital but have no idea who you are. (I only suffered a spinal cord injury; is it too late to pound my head against a brick wall?)

Luckily my greater appreciation of sick humor hasn't spoiled the pleasure I find in humor of the less cynical kind. Over the years I've enjoyed many moments of

simple delight. One morning Dana and I were awakened at about 5:30 A.M. as three–year–old Will burst into
the bedroom with his arms extended, spinning in cir-
cles, saying, "Look! I'm a hummingbird!" One of the
highlights after my injury was Robin Williams's sudden
appearance in the ICU dressed in full scrubs, imperson-
ating a manic Russian proctologist. During one of his
many visits to our home he watched a nurse suction secretions from my trache with a coughalator, basically a
vacuum cleaner for the lungs. Robin grabbed it and
went to work on the bedspread, then the curtains, and
was about to start on the carpet before his new toy was
taken away from him.

SINCE THE BEGINNING OF MY NEW LIFE, I'VE ALWAYS
wanted it to be as normal as possible. The longing for
normalcy applies to every aspect of living with a disability, from health to relationships, work, travel, and
play. It's been difficult to find the right balance between
managing my own needs and meeting my obligations
to others. Some days I don't realize how serious and
"heavy" I am. How nice it is then to be teased. I love it
when I approach the dinner table, which I occasionally
hit as I try to park, and Will picks up his plate, warning,
"Look out for the crazy driver." Or when I tell Dana how

nice her new sweater looks and she reminds me that I bought it for her birthday three years ago.

My oldest son, Matthew, teases me relentlessly about my computer illiteracy and general ignorance of modern technology (I have to admit that when the occupational therapists tried to teach me to use a voice-activated computer in rehab I kept falling asleep). My daughter, Alexandra, refers to me as "The Big Cheese" behind my back. I take that as a compliment, an affirmation for her and our whole family that I'm still an authority figure and worthy of the respect they've always shown me. Most important, all three of my children have a great sense of humor. Will has a very dry wit and understands double meanings that would go right over the heads of many nine-year-olds. Matthew and Al, now twenty-two and eighteen respectively, enjoy humor ranging from *The Osbournes* to sophisticated exchanges with adults and their friends in college. It's a great relief to see that my disability doesn't seem to be holding them back.

Perhaps the best piece of advice about humor came from a complete stranger who wrote, "Laugh now, so you don't end up living in the past." When people ask me, "How do you keep it together?" my answer is, "Mostly with duct tape." It keeps the hose from falling off the ventilator that keeps me alive; it's good for taping pieces of the armrests on my chair back together after I've crashed into something; I use it to put Will's artwork up on our walls. Chamois (our beloved yellow Lab) loves to chase rolls of duct tape when she gets tired of tennis balls. The company that makes it should use me in a commercial.

The emotional extremes of adjusting to a catastrophic illness or disability range from suicidal despair to recovering an appetite for life. Somewhere in between is a gray area of numbness. You don't feel really depressed but you don't get excited about anything either. One day blends into another as the same rituals of care are repeated over and over again. You think about calling a friend but decide not to because there's not much to say. Often you have to be persuaded to go outdoors by a nurse or family member who reminds you that you've been sitting in your office without moving for more than six hours. You hear of a recent experiment in a laboratory described as "an exciting breakthrough": paralyzed rats treated with X were able to climb a few steps up a rope ladder six weeks later. You think, "Terrific. What does it mean to me or any of the rest of us?"

In my new life I've slipped into that "numb zone" many times. That's when creating humor and appreciating it becomes very difficult, but even more necessary.

It doesn't matter if you're not that funny. (As a friend of Robin Williams for nearly thirty years I learned that lesson long ago.) The point is that the numb zone can become dangerously comfortable. If you get stuck in it for a long period of time you may end up going back to square one, when life after a catastrophe has no meaning.

I'm reminded of a legendary show-business anecdote about a comedian lying on his deathbed. When asked how he was feeling, he replied, "Dying is easy; comedy is hard." Many of us live in the numb zone whether we are disabled or not. In fact many people who are suffering from some condition look at others who are not ill but seem to be unhappy and wonder what gives them the right to complain. Everything's relative; no one gets to corner the market on misery. But I agree with the dying comedian: sometimes humor is hard, but it's worth it.

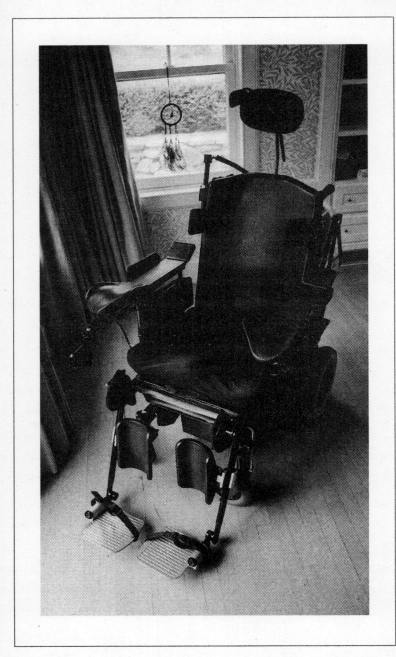

Mind/Body

When I was injured I thought that it must be my fault, that I was being punished for being a bad person. That's a natural reaction. But part of what helped me to turn around fairly quickly was the core of discipline I had developed over the years. It helped me to see this as a new chapter in my life rather than the end of it.

—*Remarks at the Kennedy Center,*
Greater Washington Society of Association Executives
Distinguished Speaker Series, December 2, 1996

There is great treasure there behind our skull and this is true about all of us. This little treasure has great, great powers, and I would say we only have learned a very, very small part of what it can do.

—*Isaac Bashevis Singer*

Before my injury I believed that our overall health is affected by our state of mind, but I was highly skeptical of those claiming to be healers. The damage to my spinal cord and all the ensuing complications led to a reconsideration of those beliefs. I've had pneumonia, blood clots, broken bones, and reactions to drugs—which have all required medical care ranging from pills to IV antibiotics to hospitalization. I've also been approached by many well-meaning individuals who have professed the ability to heal me noninvasively, using only their "special powers."

An emergency, such as a blood clot or a collapsed lung, has always led me immediately to the ER. Long-term issues of gaining strength and recovery of function have made me wonder if there are indeed genuine healers who can, as they claim, effect change simply by touch. Most have been easy to dismiss because their claims of past success seemed dubious at best and their proposals for treating me sounded very far-fetched.

But twice I let my guard down and allowed myself to be examined and treated. The first healer arrived from Ireland—a short, friendly character in his late fifties wearing a bright green jacket. My first thought was that a leprechaun had come to save me. He claimed that acupressure along my spinal cord would release endorphins that would relieve the pain and create "a new environment." I told him that there was no pain, but that didn't seem to faze him in the least. Suddenly my right arm twitched and moved a few inches. He immediately took credit, but everyone in the room knew that it was only a routine spasm—an involuntary movement caused by nerves seeking a connection to the brain. Score: Medicine 1, Healer 0.

Supernatural health provider number two actually made a house call. (Try getting a regular doctor to do that.) He had been recommended by an acquaintance who told me that he had successfully cured people of ulcers and cancer, as well as one spinal cord injury. Will answered the doorbell, and down the hall came a banker or a stockbroker in his mid-thirties, dressed in conventional business attire. My first thought was, "I'm glad he has a day job." He accepted a glass of water and settled into a chair in my office. I soon learned that he *had* been in the business world until he was "called" to change his life's work (though apparently not his wardrobe) five years earlier. He began his assessment of me by looking at my hands and noticing that the little finger on the left was broken. I told him that it was an old fracture from a family soccer game and I'd never bothered to have it set. He announced that we should do "first things first" and that he would heal the finger right away. I sat silently for over an hour with my eyes closed because I didn't want to disrupt his concentration. He massaged the finger, kneaded it, moved it in all directions, but kept trying to start a conversation. How did I like living out in the country? Any new film projects? I see (looking at a picture of our boat on the wall) that you're a sailor. Me too! I kept my answers short, instinctively not wanting to give him too much information. At last he announced that he was done. I looked down and saw that indeed the little finger was lying flat on the armrest of my chair instead of in its usual contracted position. I have to admit I was pretty impressed—especially because, like the leprechaun, he didn't charge anything for the session. We made plans for another visit the next week. But even before he had reached the front door on his way out, my finger began to curl up again. It has remained that way ever since. (It

seems that both times I got what I paid for.) Score: Medicine 2, Healers 0.

In the quest for a cure from disease or relief from
psychological and emotional distress, you could put
pure medicine at one end of the spectrum and supernatural interventions at the other. I've always been fascinated by the possibility that the treatment for disease
and the cause of disease lie somewhere in the middle. I
share the widely held belief that there is a relationship
between the mind and the body that can both create a
physical condition and enable us to recover from it.

As a teenager I suffered from occasional asthma
and a variety of allergies. For some reason the worst at-
tacks came on when I went to visit my father. Was that
because of mold spores or mildew or the tall grass
around his nineteenth-century farmhouse? A few of my
friends near my home in New Jersey lived in similar
houses, but I never had a reaction when I visited them.
The only logical explanation had to be that I was extremely anxious to please my father. It was difficult to
relax, be myself, or literally "breathe easy" when he was
around. Since these issues were never discussed, it
might have been tension building up inside that often
left me gasping for breath and sneaking off to use my
inhaler.

Perhaps the level of stress in the mind determines

the severity of its manifestation in the body. There is overwhelming evidence that stress can be linked to hypertension, ulcers, and a compromised immune system. Many researchers agree that some forms of cancer are caused or made worse by repressed anger. When President Nixon was embroiled in the Watergate scandal in 1973, he faced the nation and told us, even as beads of sweat formed above his lip, "I am not a crook." At the same time he developed phlebitis—a condition that causes pain and swelling due to partially blocked circulation—in one leg. Was this a coincidence, or was it caused by the mental stress of maintaining a cover-up? Whenever we don't feel well we tend to blame it on external causes: the weather, contact with others, the environment, or even something we ate. These may well be contributing factors, but we should acknowledge that the source of many ailments is within ourselves.

If we accept that the mind/body connection can produce harmful effects, then we can assume that the same connection has a healing power as well. Before my injury, a positive attitude probably helped me bounce back from various injuries and illnesses. But nothing that had gone before could have prepared me for an experience I had two years after I was paralyzed.

In the spring of 1997 a small red spot appeared on my left ankle, probably caused by irritation from my shoe. Within a month the red spot had become a serious wound. It was only an inch and a half wide, but the skin had broken down, layer after layer, until the anklebone itself was exposed. Then the site became infected and turned septic as it spread up my leg. I was examined by specialists and told that there was the potential for a systemic infection, which might prove fatal. If they detected any indications of that scenario the only recourse would be to amputate my leg above the knee. I remember my immediate reaction, which I did not hesitate to share with the experts: I told them that was absolutely unacceptable, because I would need my leg in order to walk. I remember mentally drawing a line in the sand, establishing a barrier that could not and would not be crossed.

I was put on a ten-day course of a powerful antibiotic administered intravenously. As I sat on the porch of our summer home in Massachusetts, gazing for hours on end at the hills surrounding our property, I kept picturing my ankle as it used to be. Slowly but surely new layers of skin began to form. Six months later the wound had closed. Within a year the ankle appeared perfectly normal.

I don't claim to understand precisely why my wound healed and my leg was saved. Certainly Fortaz, the prescribed antibiotic, is an aggressive therapy. But even the strongest antibiotics don't always work; I had learned that from other treatments when I was in rehab. Looking back at it now, I believe that I wouldn't have recovered without the drug. But I also believe that I wouldn't have recovered without an ironclad agreement between my mind and my body that I had to keep my leg.

There were many times during the healing process when I still felt very anxious about the outcome. It was much like the decision not to commit suicide after my accident—the decision created consequences of hard work, sacrifice, and the beginning of a journey into the unknown. It was relatively easy to tell the doctors that I would refuse amputation; my response was instinctive and probably irrational, driven by my aggressive and competitive personality. It was far more difficult to sit on the porch with my leg propped up on pillows constantly trying to push doubt and negativity out of my mind. One minute I would think, "I can do this—I can heal this wound." The next minute I would think, "What are you talking about? You don't have any special powers." Then I would try yet again to picture my ankle as it used to be and tell myself that it deserved to be whole. I reminded myself that I had always recovered from all kinds of setbacks. There was even good reason to believe that sooner or later my spinal cord could be repaired and the nightmare of paralysis would be over. Why shouldn't this ankle come with me as I moved forward?

Internal chatter after a brave decision is probably the rule rather than the exception. When a field commander gives his troops the order "Follow me!" he might be extremely anxious or downright terrified. But he has to project confidence and authority, or the troops will only reluctantly do their duty without rallying behind him. In some cases the old adage "Fake it until you make it" is actually helpful. You make a choice or set a goal and let people know about it. Then just getting started leads to the discovery of internal resources that help us go farther than we ever thought we could.

My friend David Blaine is perhaps the best example of an individual who has used those internal resources to go farther than ordinary people can imagine. A slender, soft-spoken young man, he performs unbelievable magic with an air of nonchalance that almost borders on lethargy. But what sets him apart are his feats of endurance. He has been buried alive, frozen in a block of ice, and most recently, in May 2002, he stood on top of an eighty-foot pole for thirty-four hours before jumping into a pile of cardboard boxes. He has been described as a thrill seeker, a nut case, a guy who will do anything for publicity and money. As someone trying to overcome the limitations of a disability, which requires exercise and discipline, I take exception to those who so readily dismiss his achievements.

The truth about David is that he was pushing the limits of his endurance long before the media had ever heard of him; that he lived for years just above the poverty line; and that he prepares for every "stunt" with rigid self-discipline. He trained for the pole for over a year, starting at twenty feet and learning from the best Hollywood stuntmen how to fall safely into airbags. Once he was comfortable standing on a twenty-two-inch platform and jumping from that height, he moved up to forty feet and gradually worked his way up to eighty. He never used a harness or a safety net. Why did he do it? Because he was always afraid of heights and wanted to free himself from that fear.

The vast majority of people live within a comfort zone that is relatively small. The comfort zone is defined by fear and our perception of our limitations. We are occasionally willing to take small steps outside it, but few of us dare to expand it. Those who dare sometimes fail and retreat, but many experience the satisfaction of moving into a larger comfort zone and the joyful anticipation of more success. A person living with a disability may find the courage to leave the comfort zone of his own house for the first time. An able-bodied individual might decide to face claustrophobia by taking up scuba diving. Even as our country tries to cope with terrorism, most of us know intuitively that living in fear is not living at all.

David's physical preparation included daily uphill climbs on a mountain bike so that he would have enough strength left in his legs to control his jump off the pole at the end of thirty-four hours. He also learned to fast for long periods of time; in fact, he didn't eat anything during the entire performance.

The most extraordinary use of his own resources was the power of his mind. He used his mind to overcome his fear of heights and to summon the willpower to go without food. His mind kept his body from failing. When he did jump, he imagined that he was falling into air mattresses, which he had done almost exclusively in practice. The result was a perfect landing.

THE VICTORY OVER THE ANKLE IN 1997 WAS A LANDMARK for me. Since then I've been much less concerned about what else could go wrong with my body. I've also found the self-discipline to exercise when I don't feel like it, which is extremely important because overall health and any hope of recovery can't be achieved without it.

I've learned to stick to a conscientious diet; keeping my weight under control makes muscular and cardiovascular conditioning much easier. Since '97 my skin has stayed intact; as a result I have the freedom to sit in my chair for as many as fourteen to fifteen hours. In the old days I was often limited to five or six. I have been able to avoid many urinary tract infections and keep the bases of my lungs functioning almost normally.

All of that is extremely hard work, and many times I don't succeed. Just recently I suffered from severe bloating of my stomach and difficulty breathing. X rays showed that huge pockets of air had formed in my large intestine, which was putting pressure on my diaphragm. The remedy didn't come from the mind/body connection; I made changes in my diet and underwent a procedure to clear the blockage.

Perhaps I am still in the early stages of learning to control manifestations in my body with the power of my mind. At this point it seems that I am able to respond to emergencies such as the threatened amputation of a limb. I get the sense that in time I will discover the ability to do more. But now I'm confident that when something comes up, when germs invade and systems fail as they inevitably do, my mind and body, with the assistance of medicine, will keep me healthy and prepared for the future.

Parenting

≡

As parents we all have different ideas of what
success means for our children. I think the most
important aspect of success has to do with
finding a real passion for something in life. It
means a responsibility to live up to one's
potential. That has to be discovered; it can't be
forced upon a youngster growing up. We cannot
expect children to be replicas of us. From the
minute they emerge from the womb they are
already themselves. That must be honored, and
they must be given the tools and opportunities
to go as far as they possibly can on their own.

—*Keynote address,*
Brown University Parents' Weekend, October 2001

When I was born in September 1952, my father, Franklin, was only twenty-four. Although our relationship was always complex—and became increasingly complicated as I moved into adulthood—as a youngster I delighted in the fact that he was young too. Because he was a college professor, first at Columbia, then at Wesleyan and Yale, his vacations generally coincided with ours. My brother, Ben, and I, my half-brothers Brock and Mark, and my half-sister, Alison, all cherished his attention and the activities we shared with him when we were very young.

During the Christmas holidays he taught us to ski. He and my stepmother, Helen, bought a tiny cottage in Ludlow, Vermont, close to several ski areas. All five children were on the slopes by age three and skiing on our own by four or five. Once we were on top of the mountain we waited together as my father stationed himself a hundred yards below. When he was ready we skied down to him one at a time until we were all assembled for his review. Then he would go another hundred yards down the slope and we would repeat the process until we reached the bottom.

He had a special talent for communicating with each child based on age and skill. I was the oldest and Mark was the youngest, a difference of nearly ten years, with the others spaced fairly evenly in between. For all of us, a word of praise could make our day. On the other hand, because he thought the lift tickets (about $10) were outrageously expensive, we had to be the first ones on the mountain and the last to leave, which could make for a miserable day. Once the tickets were bought we *skied*, weather and snow conditions notwithstanding, with a thirty-minute break for the bathroom and lunch. (I don't recall any of us ever complaining about the cold or asking to go in early for a cup of hot chocolate.) But we all became expert skiers; Alison qualified to be an instructor when she was only fifteen. Today, in our forties, we are still avid skiers (except me) and have passed our enthusiasm on to our children.

In the springs and summers of our childhood, Pa taught us to swim, sail, play tennis, and paddle a canoe properly—at around nine we all learned to execute a proper J–stroke, which enables one person to keep the canoe going forward in a straight line. Some of these skills were acquired at my grandmother's lakeshore house in the Pocono Mountains of Pennsylvania, others on the Connecticut River and Long Island Sound. As we grew older, we developed special interests in addition to learning the basics. Somehow Pa found time to work and play with each of us individually. Ben was fascinated by all things mechanical and electrical, so he and my father spent hours maintaining the car, an old secondhand Peugeot. As far as I remember, it never went to the shop: they repaired faulty wiring, adjusted the brakes, replaced worn shock absorbers, and gave it routine tune–ups as needed.

Mark liked baseball and beachcombing. He and Pa used to sneak up into the attic, where the old black–and–white rabbit–eared television lived in exile, to watch the Yankees. (The TV was not allowed in the living room as a precaution against bad habits.) Down in the basement the two of them created a museum where the most interesting rocks and seashells collected on cruises from Connecticut to Maine were on display.

Alison (always called Alya) and Brock were very musical. Both played the piano, and Alya played the flute as well. Pa played the recorder. Visitors who dropped by in the late afternoon or after dinner were often drawn into the house by the sound of them playing together. Brock and Alya both took riding lessons when they were still quite young. Alya eventually lost interest, but Brock carried on and still rides today. Although he wasn't a rider himself, my father used to drive them to the stables, where he watched with a critical eye at ringside as they worked with their instructor. When Alya dropped out and Brock progressed into show jumping, riding became a unique part of his relationship with our father.

My special interest was the theater. As a youngster I did well in skiing, sailing, and tennis. But by the time I was fourteen, I spent my summers first in acting workshops, then as a theater apprentice, and before long, on tour in a play or performing as a member of a repertory company. Pa generally liked my work. His critique after a show was usually kind and constructive: he was the first to point out that I often stood onstage with my knees hyperextended, which made me look tense and inhibited natural movement. After a performance of *The Complaisant Lover*, an obscure English drawing-room comedy in which I attempted to play an upper-class gentleman in his forties (I was seventeen at the time), he approved of my accent but pointed out that I obviously had no idea how to smoke a cigarette, which would be second nature for my character. However, my comic timing received high marks.

No one in our family had ever been an actor, which made me feel truly unique. Pa particularly enjoyed productions in theaters not too far from the water so he could get there on *Pandion*, our twenty-six-foot Pearson sloop. That worked out pretty well: one summer I worked in Boston, another in Boothbay, Maine, and one tour played in four theaters on Cape Cod. It wasn't until I left postgraduate studies at Juilliard and entered the commercial world of film and television that acting became a source of contention between us. As a pure academic, he cherished the theater as a place for language and ideas. He was never very interested in film, even as an art form, and had nothing but contempt for television (except as an outlet for the Yankees).

I'm very grateful that he supported me as I began to learn my trade, and that, for a time, we shared something unique. Without his encouragement in the early years I don't know if I would have developed the self-confidence to attempt such a challenging career.

MY OLDER SON, MATTHEW, WAS BORN IN 1979, WHEN I was twenty-seven. I wanted to be a father while I was still young so that I could be actively and physically involved with my children for a long time. I wanted to teach them things firsthand and introduce them to a wide variety of activities and subjects, and then give them the freedom to pick and choose as they grew up. Alexandra came along when I was thirty-one. Then there was a long gap until Will made his entrance in 1992, just a few months before my fortieth birthday, when I still considered myself to be a relatively young dad.

I started activities with all three at an early age just as my father had done. Matthew and Al were out on the slopes learning to snowplow by four or five. Will started playing hockey in the living room with the cap of an apple juice jar and a little plastic golf club when he was two. Over time they developed unique talents and interests that both set them apart and bound us together. Matthew loved tennis, fishing, and movies. Alexandra learned to ride. During the filming of *The Remains of the Day* in 1992, she and I used to gallop across the English countryside on magnificent hunters, courtesy of the Duke of Beaufort. She learned to play the bassoon when the instrument was almost bigger than she was. We used to play duets, with me at the piano. When we were satisfied with the sound of a piece we would perform it for the family and add it to our repertoire.

One of the reasons I enjoyed being a young father so much was that I had plenty of energy and great enthusiasm. I loved suggesting activities on the spur of the moment. I might challenge Matthew to a game of chess or announce that it was time to put on boots and go for a hike. If the wind dropped to nothing when we were sailing offshore, I used to dive overboard and try to coax everyone else to jump in. Matthew and Al always worried that an unknown creature from the deep would come up to the surface and get them. It was very hard to convince them otherwise, especially after the day an enormous basking shark rose to sunbathe just as I was climbing aboard for another dive.

The list of activities we shared was long and I tried to make our interaction a two–way street; they might approach me or I might approach them with ideas. And we could touch. There were always lots of hugs, pats on the back, rides on my shoulders, pillow fights, and games of tag. The rituals of baths and curling up together to read at bedtime, putting Band–Aids on both real and imaginary wounds—all these and more helped to give them a foundation of security, which every child needs.

And then, in an instant, the moment my head hit the hard ground in Culpeper, Virginia, everything changed. Or so I believed. As I lay in bed in the ICU, I concluded that I could no longer be a real father to my three children. I assumed that my new life as a quadriplegic would not only mark the end of the life we had known, but cause enormous psychological and emotional damage to them as well. How could I relate to them if we couldn't do things together? How would we adjust to the loss of spontaneity? What kind of a father would I be if I literally couldn't reach out to them, if I was always going back to the hospital, if a nurse had to be on duty 24/7?

The answers started to come within weeks of the accident, in the summer of '95. Matthew and Al stayed in a local hotel and visited me every day. (Will came with Dana or our nanny almost every day as well.) I kept telling them that I was okay, and that they should go enjoy the summer instead of hanging around a depressing rehab center. But they wanted to be with me. Even if they could only see me two or three hours each visit, they wanted to be nearby.

We spent most of the time talking. I quickly realized that we'd never really done that before. When Matthew and Al flew over from England to be with Dana and me for at least a part of every vacation, I usually picked them up at the airport in Boston. Then it was a three-hour drive across Massachusetts to our home in the Berkshires. I remember listening to the radio together on one of those trips when they were about nine and five. We tuned in to a variety of stations that played classical music, rock 'n' roll, contemporary top forty, and oldies. I asked them to identify the meter: Was the piece in 1/2, 3/4, 4/4, 6/8, or something else? How would they describe the tempo of the classical pieces:

adagio, andante, allegro, or something else? In the rock 'n' roll and contemporary pop selections could they distinguish between the main melody and the bridge, also known as the middle eight? Somewhere along the Mass Pike, Al piped up in her chirpy English accent. "Do you know, Daddy," she said, "this is the first time in such a long time that we've had a real conversation about something?" I realized that she was right. Not that we didn't talk, but usually it was while doing something else. Now I gave them my full attention, and I soon learned to listen more than talk. That began a process of discovering that, in bringing up children and relating to others, sometimes *being* is more important than *doing*. I was also to learn that even if you can't move, you can have a powerful effect with what you say.

One special day in Will's life is a good example. When he was six, he was still afraid to ride by himself without the training wheels on his bike. Dana spent hours killing her back as she bent over to hold his seat as he pedaled around timidly in front of our garage. I decided to see if I could help. I told him to start with his left foot on the ground and to set the right pedal in the fully raised position. I told him to grab the handlebars, push hard on the right pedal, and then put his left foot on the other pedal and keep going, being careful not to oversteer. I said if he kept his hands steady the bike wouldn't wobble so much. He listened carefully and got into the ready position. Then he froze, afraid to make that first push. I told him to take his time, but added that I was prepared to sit in the driveway all afternoon until he did it. I reminded him that I would never ask him to do any- thing too scary or too difficult. He didn't complain; he just sat there for quite a long time assessing the situation. Then I announced that on the count of three he should start. I made it a long count, but after three I said, "Go," and he did it. He pushed down, the bike moved forward, he got his other foot on the pedal, and off he went. On his first run he made a complete circle around the drive- way. As he came past my chair the first time, his face was a study in fierce concentration. The second time he came by, he was smiling. For the next fifteen minutes he kept riding around our circular drive, gradually picking up speed. After that he wanted to go down the steep hill toward our mailbox, but we saved that for another day.

If someone had told me before my injury that you could teach a kid to ride on his own just by talking to him, I would have said that was impossible. Timing is very important: words can only have a positive effect on others if and when they are ready to listen. And we have to choose our words carefully, particularly when we are the voice of authority for people who are vulnerable. In the first weeks after my injury, I was like a child and the doctors seemed like parents, while the nurses became older brothers and sisters. I hung on every word and tried to interpret the expressions on their faces. Everything they said and did had an enormous impact on me. I remembered all of it; sometimes I replayed scenes over and over in my head. When I was told that my spinal cord had been severed and I would never recover any sensation or movement below my shoulders, I was haunted by those words for months. When I was told that was incorrect, my spirits rose again with the possibility that I was on the road to recovery.

The experience of feeling like a child gave me a new perspective on being a father. I became acutely aware that virtually everything that parents say and do has a powerful effect on our children, even when we think they're not paying attention. We have to constantly monitor the level of communication and be ready to take action if a child is tuning us out or having difficulty expressing his or her feelings. During Matthew's freshman year in college we had a few awkward phone conversations. He didn't sound like himself. Even though he said everything was all right, I could sense that he was telling me what he thought I wanted to hear. I invited him to come down for the weekend just to hang out and maybe go into the city for dinner or a Rangers game. My real agenda was for us to spend time alone. On Sunday afternoon we sat together in my office for nearly four hours. I began the conversation simply by asking him to tell me everything that was on his mind. I told him he could say anything and I promised not to interrupt him.

The floodgates opened, perhaps because I removed any resistance he might have been expecting. He covered issues ranging from problems with his professors, other students, the challenges of college life in general, to aspects and moments of his childhood that he had never brought up with me before. I was surprised by much of what he said, particularly with regard to our relationship. I suggested that a tendency to be too polite might have been the source of a communications breakdown when he and Al were young. Time and again I would ask either one of them what they would like to do and get the same response: "I don't mind." Often we ended up doing what I wanted to do and they dutifully tagged along on long bike rides, mountain hikes, and offshore sailing in foul weather. When I asked them if everything was okay, the usual reply, even through their teenage years, was "Fine."

As Matthew went on that Sunday afternoon I realized I could have done a better job reading between the lines. As I listened I reminded myself that none of us has the right to refute someone else's experience or perception. If a child says that when a parent did X or said

Y it caused him pain, the parent must not say that it isn't true. I think we should explore what happened and try to find out what caused that feeling. The worst thing we can do is to say, "That's wrong, you're exaggerating, you're rewriting history." Many times the only thing to say, as long as we really mean it, is "I'm sorry."

I believe that becoming a parent is a gift, even though parenting means taking on an enormous responsibility. It's a miracle that a child can come into the world and instinctively give us unconditional love. If we can return that kind of love and provide a nurturing environment, the responsibility becomes less challenging. I was on my feet when Matthew and Al were born, and thought I was ready to be a good parent; certainly I would try to make their childhood in some ways different than mine. For the first two years of Will's life, all was well. The children were thriving, and I felt the privilege much more than the responsibility.

When I decided to live my new life, the weight of responsibility was suddenly overwhelming. But because all three were a vital part of that decision, simply by showing (as Dana did) that they loved me as much as always, I was able to overcome feelings of guilt and inadequacy, which actually made me a better father. I'm very grateful for that, although I wish I could have learned the lesson the hard way.

Religion

When I do good I feel good.

When I do bad I feel bad.

And that's my religion.

—*Abraham Lincoln, 1860*

During the last few years countless numbers of people have remarked, "Your faith must be a great help as you cope with your ordeal." Then they ask, "What is your religion?" That used to put me in an awkward position, because I could tell they wanted to hear that I am a deeply religious person. The truth is that I only found a religion very recently that I can reconcile with a lifelong quest for the meaning of spirituality.

Religious studies were integrated into the core curriculum when I was in the eighth grade at Princeton (New Jersey) Day School. Religion was also mandatory in ninth grade; after that it was optional. The two-year course was an introduction to the world's religions, and the history of those religions most closely associated with contemporary American culture. I enjoyed learn-

ing some of the basic precepts of Eastern religions such
as Taoism, Shintoism, and Buddhism. I liked the idea
that all living things are sacred and that there are gods
in trees, flowers, the earth, water, and sky. But I found
many of the teachings and much of the history of West-
ern religions quite disturbing. In my early teens I sang
in the choir of the Presbyterian church, and was intimidated by frightening images projected by some of the
hymns: "God the Father Almighty"; "Onward Christian
Soldiers Marching as to War"; "the fateful lightning of
His terrible swift sword."

It seemed to me that this God probably loves us—
His children—but uses scare tactics to keep us in line. If
we are virtuous and righteous in His eyes, we are safe.
He will protect us and deliver us from evil. But if we
transgress or simply fail to live up to His expectations,
we will be punished accordingly. That dynamic too
closely resembled my relationship with my own father;
why would I voluntarily choose to re-create it?

Occasionally I attended Sunday school before the
main service in an attempt to broaden my perspective
and to please my stepfather, Tristam Johnson, a lifelong
member of the church. Unfortunately I didn't learn
much in Sunday school because the teacher was former
senator and pro basketball star Bill Bradley, who was a

Princeton University undergraduate at the time. My friends and I often went to Mr. Bradley's home games on Saturdays and then managed to steer the conversation away from the Bible to basketball on Sunday mornings.

The religious studies in school, combined with a thirteen-year-old's burgeoning desire to butt heads with authority, continued to drive me away from organized religion. Our class learned about intolerance, oppression, persecution, and the accumulation of vast wealth by the church hierarchy at the expense of the impoverished and uneducated faithful. We learned that religion started wars, that the Great Crusades of the Middle Ages were actually imperialist conquests justified in the name of Christ. We read about sixteenth-century explorers and missionaries to the New World who believed it was their duty to claim as much land as possible for their countries and to convert the "savages" to their faith. In biology class, we learned about birth control and family planning; when we discussed contemporary Catholicism in religious studies, many of us struggled to understand it. We bombarded the teacher with questions: How can priests be marriage counselors if they've never been married? Since poor Catholics in developing countries are forbidden to use birth control, is that why they have so many large families living in terrible conditions? Aren't overpopulation and world hunger going to be huge problems when we grow up?

In addition to the influences of church and school during my formative years, my father's atheism was an important factor. Not only did I grow up without a foundation in religion, but I lacked any sense of spirituality as well. I was preoccupied by the here and now, running on ambition and self-reliance. As I moved on to college and then to New York in pursuit of an acting career, I wasn't looking for answers to the Big Questions: Why are we here? Do we have a purpose? Is there a "right" way to live?

In the fall of 1975, I was living in my own apartment on the Upper West Side and in rehearsal for *A Matter of Gravity*, a Broadway-bound play with Katharine Hepburn. I had just turned twenty-two and was rather proud of myself. And why not? I had earned a B.A. from Cornell, been a graduate student at Juilliard, appeared in several off-Broadway productions, and gained notoriety as a likable bad guy on a daytime TV series. In my spare time I was taking flying lessons and fully enjoying my life as a young bachelor in the Big Apple.

One afternoon on my way to the grocery store, I came across a young man standing next to a sign on the sidewalk that read, FREE PERSONALITY TEST, NO OBLIGATION. Figuring I had nothing to lose, I followed his directions to the sixth floor of the prewar apartment building behind him. The door was unlocked, so I opened it and found myself in the New York headquarters of the Church of Scientology.

The whole place was buzzing with energy and activity. In the main office area about thirty people were working at their desks or gathered in small groups, engaged in quiet but intense conversation. They all appeared to be in their late twenties or early thirties, ethnically diverse, clean-cut, and neat. The men wore shirts and ties and the women were dressed in modest skirts or slacks. In a far corner, six Scientologists sat facing each other in two rows of three. None of them spoke; everyone stared intently into the eyes of the person opposite. They were clearly not distracted by the ebb and flow of workers in the office behind them. I was amazed by the apparent depth of their concentration, even as I wondered what the purpose of staring at each other was.

A young man much like the one I'd met on the sidewalk, of medium height and build, wearing a crisp white shirt and a conservative pinstriped tie, came forward to greet me. He gave his name, shook my hand warmly, and never broke direct eye contact as he asked how he could help. I told him I was interested in the free personality test, to which he replied, "Of course. One moment, please." He stepped away briefly into the office area and came back with a form for me to fill out. The next thing I knew, I was seated at a desk in the reception area writing down my name, address, phone number, social security number, profession, date of birth, mother's maiden name, and more. In answer to the question "Are you affiliated with any other church?" I wrote "none."

I handed back the completed form and waited while he looked it over and conferred with several of his colleagues in the office. They must have reached a consensus fairly quickly because in just a few moments he came back with another form, which turned out to be the actual personality test. He invited me to return to my seat and respond to all the questions carefully, thoughtfully, and truthfully, taking as much time as I liked. There were no right or wrong answers.

As I looked over the test, I wished it were multiple choice. I wasn't expecting to have to write twenty short essays about myself. I wondered who would grade the paper: Was there an official tester who was solely responsible for evaluating the personality of every passerby who came in the door? I reminded myself that the test was free and there was no obligation, so why not just fill in the blanks, get the results, and make a quick exit.

It turned out not to be quite so easy. I spent forty-five minutes actually trying to do my very best. When I turned the test in to my host, I thought I had submitted quite an objective assessment of myself. What more could I do, especially considering that there were no right or wrong answers?

I had hoped to get the results that afternoon, but I was told that there wasn't enough time for them to review my test before the office closed for the day; I would have to come back tomorrow, but not before eleven A.M. Luckily my call time for rehearsal the next day wasn't until after lunch, so I was free to return. In hindsight, I wish my rehearsal call had been first thing in the morning.

I appeared at the church at the appropriate time, even though I wasn't sure why. Probably it was my competitive nature coming to the forefront once again: I needed to know the score. I thought I had hit a home run, so I probably just wanted to stop by for congratulations. Wrong. The same host greeted me just as warmly as he had the day before. Then I was invited to follow him. He led me down a hall and into a plush, well-appointed private office; this was obviously the inner sanctum of the headquarters, suitable for the president or CEO of a major corporation.

Before I had much time to take in my surroundings, in came three apparently heavy hitters of the organization. They shook my hand in turn and introduced themselves with the warmth and direct eye contact that I was now beginning to recognize as a trademark of Scientology. We settled into comfortable chairs and then one of the senior officials (I've forgotten his title), in a perfectly cheerful tone of voice, gave me the bad news. There was no score, no grade, no quantitative measurement, just their assessment: I was obviously deeply depressed, suffering from low self-esteem, and carrying heavy "baggage" around with me, not only from emotional damage in this incarnation but from previous lives as well. His strong recommendation—echoed by his associates, and my host as well—was that I should begin "training" immediately.

I've always been very vulnerable to criticism, so what was said at that meeting had a strong effect. Maybe my life was all an illusion and I had no true knowledge about myself—or anything else for that matter. I agreed to come back before rehearsal the next day, and to begin studying Scientology with an open mind.

The basic principles of the religion, described in the works of its founder, L. Ron Hubbard, struck me as log-

ical and highly motivating. An engineer by trade, Hubbard viewed the human mind as a complex but man-
ageable computer. Every thought, every emotion, every
experience is stored in the memory banks of the computer within us. What stops us from experiencing joy
and achieving success is that we are not "Clear": all the
negativity—self-hatred, anger, jealousy, pessimism, feelings of inadequacy, and the like—that remains in the
computer brings us down. Unless that negativity is
"blown away" we are "stuck," condemned to repeating
the same mistakes, falling into counterproductive pat-
terns of behavior and unable to find fulfillment.

No one at the church was willing to estimate how
long it would take for me to "go Clear," but they implied
that it would require quite some time. The first step was
joining a group like the one I'd seen when I first entered the headquarters, staring intently into the eyes of
another recruit sitting opposite me. The objective was
to empty our minds of extraneous thoughts ("clutter")
and focus all our attention on the other person. As we
became completely absorbed in this exercise, known as
"TR–0" (Training Routine Zero), we were to lose awareness of ourselves. Whenever our own clutter tried to
come back in, we were not to be "upset"; we were to acknowledge its return and then command it to go away.
At first this was nearly impossible. My head was filled

with nothing but clutter, unwanted thoughts about myself, and judgmental thoughts about my partner. Gradually I learned—much like someone studying Transcendental Meditation—to empty my mind. Then I was able to share the same space with another person, not doing anything, just existing. I have to admit that was quite a high. I left those early sessions, which sometimes lasted over an hour, feeling both relaxed and energized.

The TR-0 experience was relatively inexpensive, costing perhaps a few hundred dollars. But the next step was "auditing," which was outrageously expensive and would have to continue for an unspecified length of time. The church required a deposit of $3,000 in advance of one-on-one meetings with an "auditor," which cost $100 an hour. (In 1975, even the best psychoanalysts charged about half that in private practice.)

Having been convinced that I needed auditing, I put down my deposit and began meeting with my assigned auditor twice a week. She turned out to be a very attractive brunette about my age who had recently come to New York from somewhere in the Midwest. She had gone Clear and become a certified auditor in her home state, arriving not only with these credentials but the bright-eyed enthusiasm of a hostess at Disneyland.

We worked together seated on opposite sides of a wide mahogany desk. In front of her was an "E-Meter," a simple box with a window that contained a fluctuating needle and a card with numbers from one to ten. Two wires running out of the box and across the desk were attached to tin cans that I was asked to hold, one in each hand. As my auditor asked questions my responses would translate into electrical impulses that flowed through the cans and the wires, causing the needle to move. The E-Meter was basically a crude lie detector. Questions touching issues that needed to be "blown away" would peg the needle at ten; anything innocuous hardly registered. I remember feeling a little foolish, but I had already invested a huge amount of money so I had to give it a chance.

One of the reasons that auditing was such a long and expensive process for most people in training was that we had to recall the use of almost every kind of drug. Not just illegal substances, but painkillers, antibiotics, routine vaccinations such as flu shots—anything and everything stronger than aspirin. Hubbard believed that a student could not go Clear without completely deleting drugs from the mind's computer. Obviously it's crucial for anyone to kick a drug habit, but why would he object to penicillin or a vaccination against measles?

(Fortunately there was no list of forbidden foods, and we didn't have to remember every cigarette or sip of beer.)

My drug rundown used up four or five sessions, and then it was on to past lives. I was asked to go back as far as I could to try to remember my earliest incarnation. We all began as souls, or "Thetans," floating somewhere in space, until we entered a body at some time in history. Sitting across from my auditor and holding the tin cans lightly (I had learned that gripping them too hard caused sweaty palms and false readings on the E-Meter), I searched the back rooms of my mind. Nothing there. Several minutes of agonizing silence went by as my auditor waited patiently.

Then my growing skepticism about Scientology and my training as an actor took over. With my eyes closed, I gradually began to remember details from a devastating past life experience that had happened in ancient Greece. I was the commander of a warship returning victoriously to Athens after a battle in Crete. My father was the king and I was his only son, the sole heir to the throne. Many months before, when my fleet cast off from the port city of Piraeus, he had embraced me and made me promise one thing: on our return we would set white sails for victory, and black sails in memoriam if I had been defeated or lost at sea.

After our glorious triumph we departed the coast of Crete at night, carrying our black sails to slip away unnoticed. As a fair wind pushed us quickly homeward, on board the celebrations began. There was wine, music, dancing, and tributes to the gods. I allowed the men to eat freely; there was no more need for rationing because we would soon be home.

On the morning of the third day we could make out the shores of Greece and the city of Piraeus in the distance. Lookouts on a promontory saw our ships; messengers were sent to fetch the king. He arrived with great fanfare within the hour, hastened to the best vantage point, and eagerly searched the horizon. By now the ships were in plain view, but the sight of them was devastating to the king: they were fast approaching Piraeus, but all were flying black sails. Carried away by the joyous celebration of victory on the voyage home, I had neglected to give the order to change them. The king, my beloved father, in despair over the loss of his son, threw himself off the promontory into the sea and died instantly.

The auditors are trained to listen to the students without emotion; their job is to write down what is said and record the indications of the needle on the E–Meter. But I could tell that my auditor was deeply moved by my story and trying hard to maintain her professional demeanor. I sensed that she was making a profound connection between guilt over the death of my father when I was a Greek warrior in a past life and my relationship with my father in the present.

And that was the end of my training as a Scientologist. My story was actually a slightly modified account of an ancient Greek myth: Theseus' return to his homeland after slaying the Minotaur in Crete. According to legend, his father, King Aegeus, was in fact so distraught by the sight of the black sails that he plunged to his death in the waters known ever after as the Aegean Sea. I didn't expect my auditor to be familiar with Greek mythology; I was simply relying on her ability, assisted by the E-Meter, to discern the truth. The fact that I got away with a blatant fabrication completely devalued my belief in the process.

Of course that was 1975, and my case may have been an exception to the rule. Many well-known and highly respected people credit Scientology for success in their careers, in relationships, and especially in their family lives. I fully support whatever belief systems make us better human beings. My problem has always been with religious dogma intended to manipulate behavior, and a claim by any religion that theirs is the One True Way.

The end of my encounter with Scientology marked the beginning of an ongoing search for the meaning of spirituality in my life. It would take many years, many well-intentioned but misguided detours, and ultimately a near-fatal accident for me to find the answer.

Advocacy

So many of our dreams at first seem impossible, then they seem improbable, and then, when we summon the will, they soon become inevitable. If we can conquer outer space, we should be able to conquer inner space too—the frontier of the brain, the central nervous system, and all the afflictions of the body that destroy so many lives and rob our country of so much potential.

—From my speech at the Democratic National Convention, August 1996

We cannot be a strong nation unless we are a healthy nation.

—Franklin Delano Roosevelt, 1940

During the summer of 1995, the doctors and staff at the Kessler Institute in New Jersey worked tirelessly to stabilize my physical condition. The leader of the team was Dr. Steven Kirshblum, one of the most dedicated and compassionate physicians I've ever met. Every day he was the first to arrive at the rehab center and one of the last to leave. I especially enjoyed his departure routine on Friday nights. An Orthodox Jew, his faith requires him to be home by sundown. By trial and error he had found that if he ran at a certain pace on a dry sidewalk he could reach his front door in seven minutes. Rain, snow, and slippery conditions required a slight adjustment. As far as I know he always made it, even if it meant treating a patient and looking at his watch at the same time. He is very slight, only about five foot nine. And even though he was still in his early thirties when I was at Kessler, he always stood with his back curved and his shoulders slouched. I told him with mock severity that on behalf of all of us in wheelchairs, the least he could do was stand up straight. When someone told me that he had played on the varsity basketball team in college at Seton Hall, I was shocked. One more example that nothing is impossible.

The medical issues that plagued me throughout that summer—severe anemia, pneumonia, infections, and skin breakdowns—were mostly under control by mid-October. It was time to think about the outside world. That meant modifying our home for accessibility, responding to a barrage of requests by the media, and defining my role as an advocate for research and the quality of life for people with disabilities.

Advocacy soon became my top priority. It began with a visit from a businessman and a scientist. Arthur Ullian, a real estate developer from Boston, had hit a rock and flipped over the handlebars of his bicycle, leaving him paralyzed from the chest down. Still in his early forties, he had already spent four years in a wheelchair and devoted much of his time to roaming the halls of Congress in search of any representative who would listen to him. His mission was "NIH × 2": he believed that because it was classified as an "orphan condition" the National Institutes of Health would not fund spinal cord research adequately unless their budget was doubled. He wanted to achieve that goal within the next five years. With his charm and persistence he managed to open some doors, but came away empty-handed.

The scientist was Dr. Wise Young, who was both young (mid-thirties) and wise (a true pioneer in spinal cord research). In the early eighties he was instrumental in the development of methylprednisilone, a steroid that generally reduces inflammation at the site of injury by about 20 percent if it is administered within the first eight hours. In 1995 he led a team of researchers at New York University, but he was constantly distracted from his work by the pressing need to obtain more funding. At the time he was one of the few scientists who were absolutely convinced that the damaged spinal cord could be repaired. Arthur Ullian shared that conviction; the challenge was to convince the government, foundations, and investors in the private sector.

As we huddled together in a corner of the visitors' room at Kessler, they drove home the point that they had gone as far as they could go. It would take the leadership of a public figure to raise awareness and make a difference in the lives of victims without a voice. I told them I would learn as much as I could about the history and the promise of research and do whatever I could to help.

But before I could take on greater issues, Dana and I had to cope with the realities of health insurance. Dr. Kirshblum and the Kessler administration decided with us that I would be discharged on December 13. Our insurance carrier accepted that decision but notified us that the company would only pay for forty-eight days of nursing care after I returned home. I was (and still am) dependent on a ventilator 24/7 and am unable to eat, wash, or go to the bathroom by myself. What did they expect us to do after forty-eight days? The company simply refused to answer the question; we were entitled to forty-eight days, period. We requested a backup ventilator for obvious safety reasons, but were denied. The case manager said that if my ventilator failed, Dana or another family member should use an ambu bag to keep me alive until a replacement vent arrived from a supplier in the town of Hawthorne, New York. (An ambu bag is a soft plastic balloon with a fitting that attaches to the patient's trachea; someone has to squeeze it every five seconds to pump air into the lungs.) Hawthorne is a forty-five-minute drive from our home, and the manager of the medical store lives in another town about an hour away from there. He has the only set of keys and is the only one authorized to sign out equipment after hours. The worst-case scenario would be a vent failure at three A.M. with Will asleep upstairs. Without a nurse on duty Dana would never be able to leave the house overnight, which would prevent her from going on business trips that provided much-needed income. She would have to wake up, figure out that the vent had failed, connect the ambu bag, and squeeze it with one hand while trying to reach the office manager on her cell phone with the other. If Will, whose bedroom was directly above our temporary quarters in the dining room, were to wake up and cry because of all the commotion, Dana couldn't go up to comfort him. If anything else were to go wrong—such as an episode of dysreflexia, which can cause a heart attack or stroke if not treated immediately—we would be out of luck, because Dana couldn't abandon the ambu bag. Considering all the necessary steps, Dana would have to keep me alive for at least three hours until I was hooked up and breathing on a new vent.

During negotiations with our insurance carrier we discovered the main reason patients are routinely denied even the essentials: only 30 percent fight back. Since 70 percent of their policyholders are easily intimidated, there is no upside for compliance. Moral responsibility does not drive the insurance industry. Threatened lawsuits are often necessary to get results.

We didn't have to go that far. But it did take repeated "Letters of Need" from Dr. Kirshblum and the

Kessler administration, submitted and resubmitted for more than six weeks, before we were finally granted round-the-clock nursing care for the term of the policy. They never did pay for a backup vent. We bought one ourselves for $3,500 because we could afford it. (It turned out to be a more than worthwhile investment because the vent has failed a number of times over the years.) But what about others in a similar situation who simply don't have that kind of money?

Since then we have developed an excellent working relationship and have not had to lock horns with our carrier. But the solution to the nursing problem only introduced us to another one: lifetime caps. Now we were receiving the benefits we needed, but my care was (and still is) very expensive. If all we had was our primary policy, at some point we would exhaust our coverage by reaching the lifetime cap of $1 million. After that we would be on our own. Fortunately I am a member of three unions—the American Federation of Television and Radio Artists, the Screen Actors Guild, and the Directors Guild of America—which meant that $3 million of coverage was available. Most people only belong to one union or have only one privately owned policy. In the event of a catastrophic illness or disability they will probably reach the cap in less than three years. After that they often have to sell their homes or use their re-

tirement savings to afford quality care. If the care requirements continue, the end of the line is placement in
a nursing home. I think most nursing homes are merely
human parking garages: patients are maintained but
there is little or no physical therapy. The usual conse-
quence, especially for younger individuals who end up
there, is serious depression. I have not run through all
three of my insurance policies—yet.

My first political activity as a patient advocate was
an effort to raise lifetime caps. Vermont senator Jim Jef-
fords called in May 1997, asking me to support S.1114,
the Lifetime Cap Discrimination Act. We held a press
conference in June; then in July, seeking a cosponsor in
the House, I wrote a letter that was copied and hand-
delivered to all 436 members. It said, in part:

> A million dollar policy purchased in 1970 is worth
> only about $100,000 today. It is ironic that a policy
> meant to give customers peace of mind is now
> being used to force them out of the private insur-
> ance market.... It is estimated that only about
> 10,000 people will exceed their lifetime cap in the
> next five years. Raising lifetime caps will cause an
> insignificant increase in premiums (small busi-
> nesses are exempt under this legislation).... More
> than 150 organizations support this bill, which

would raise lifetime caps from $1 million to $10 million, to ensure that health insurance is there when people need it most.

The bill was defeated in the Senate, 56 to 42, probably because the majority was skeptical about the low cost of the higher premiums. Research by the sponsors had shown that the additional cost would fall somewhere between $9 and $19 annually for the average company of 250 workers. Perhaps a compromise could have been introduced that would have required employers and employees to split the cost. I've been assured a number of times that the issue will be revisited, but so far nothing has come of it.

Senators Arlen Specter (R–Pennsylvania) and Tom Harkin (D–Iowa), longtime advocates for medical research, rebounded quickly, taking a slightly different approach. They introduced S.441, the National Fund for Health Research Act. The bill proposed taking one penny from each dollar paid in insurance premiums, which would result in a nearly $6 billion increase for the National Institutes of Health. This time, I wrote to all one hundred senators:

I firmly believe that medical research is the key to eliminating disease, reducing human suffering, and lowering health care costs.... I have spoken to executives at several insurance companies about this bill and have been told that their profit margin is so small that the donation of even 1% of their income is an unreasonable hardship. I find this about as credible as the tobacco companies' claim that nicotine is not addictive. It is hard to sympathize with insurance companies when you watch a mother in tears, begging for a chair so that her quadriplegic son can take a shower.... The insurance companies see this legislation as a tax. My question is: why is it unreasonable, particularly when they would save so much money in the long run? Research will keep the American people healthier, resulting in fewer insurance claims. We tax oil companies and use the money to build and maintain highways. Most states have sales taxes, which are a major source of revenue for a wide variety of programs and services that benefit the public. Why shouldn't insurance companies be asked to help solve the health care crisis in this country?

The Harkin–Specter bill was also defeated, effectively ending the fund–raising aspect of insurance reform. Advocates for disease and disability groups returned to the campaign to double the budget of the NIH. At the invitation of Morton Kondracke, executive editor of the congressional magazine *Roll Call*, I spoke at a press conference in March 1998:

> What we've been doing is the equivalent of launching the space shuttle and then telling the astronauts, "Sorry, we didn't have enough money to fill the tank." That is the situation with the NIH today. Only 22 percent of all grant applications are being funded. There is a tremendous amount of good science that is falling by the wayside.

The next year I offered the following testimony before Congress regarding the president's budget request for the NIH in fiscal year 2000:

> Though our government operates on a budget that is decided annually, our scientists cannot. New scientific initiatives, experiments, and laboratories across the United States, once nurtured and financed, operate on two- and three- and four-year plans. We must not fund our scientists who have the potential to alleviate enormous suffering without giving them the assurance that we

will not put on the brakes and stop the flow of dollars that will make their progress possible.

... Without your support, spinal cord victims will continue to sit in wheelchairs, draining the resources of insurance companies as well as Medicaid, Medicare, VA hospitals, and nursing homes. With your continued support, it is very possible that within the next three to five years people who are now afflicted with a wide variety of disabilities will be able to overcome them. They will regain their rightful place in society, re-join the workforce, and at last be relieved of the suffering they and their families have had to en-dure. The plea for adequate funding cannot be ignored.

In the spring of 2000, the need for increased gov-ernment funding was raised exponentially by the promise of human embryonic stem cells, which have the capacity to become any cell type or tissue in the body. But researchers and patient advocates had to curb their enthusiasm in the face of strong opposition from political conservatives and religious groups. The issue became highly controversial as both sides debated the beginning of life and the morality of destroying embryos in order to obtain stem cells for research. I wrote a short essay on the subject for *Time* in June 2000:

> It is our responsibility to do everything possible to protect the quality of life of the present and future generations. A critical factor will be what we do with human embryonic stem cells.... They have been called "the body's self-repair kit."
>
> ... No obstacle should stand in the way of responsible investigation of their possibilities.... In fertility clinics, women are given a choice of what to do with unused fertilized embryos: they can be discarded, donated to research, or frozen for future use.... But why has the use of discarded embryos suddenly become such an issue? Is it more ethical for a woman to donate unused embryos that will never become human beings, or to let them be tossed away as so much garbage when they could help save thousands of lives?
>
> ... While we prolong the stem cell debate, millions continue to suffer. It is time to harness the power of government and go forward.

The ban on NIH funding of human ES cells, which went into effect almost immediately after they were first isolated at the University of Wisconsin in 1998, continued. Before he left office, President Clinton issued guidelines that were embraced by the research community and patients alike: he would allow the NIH to fund stem cell research on excess embryos freely donated from IVF (in vitro fertilization) clinics. In May 2000, S.2015, the Stem Cell Research Act of 2000, was drafted for the Senate. Once again I wrote to every member:

> Testimony from experts at NIH, letters of support from disease groups, universities, clinicians, and foundations as well as distinguished theologians have established beyond doubt that the ban on federal funding for this research must be lifted.
> ... If your young child or grandchild suddenly became paralyzed because of a spinal cord injury, or brain damaged in an accident, would you be able to look him or her in the eye and say that research on the best hope for recovery is, in the words of Senator Brownback, "illegal, immoral, and unnecessary"?

The bill remained stalled in committee and Bill Clinton left office with the ban still in effect. One of George W. Bush's first actions when he became president in January 2001 was to prohibit the adoption of the Clinton guidelines pending further review. All the interested parties held their collective breath while our new president considered the issue. We watched televised coverage of his meeting with the pope, who made it clear that the destruction of a human embryo for *any* purpose violated "the sanctity of life." The Catholic hierarchy across the country echoed the pope's position on behalf of 61 million Catholic voters. Whether or not the leaders of other faiths were given equal consideration is not clear, but many people felt it was more than inappropriate for the president to consult with any religious group: it was an outright violation of the separation of church and state. Spokesmen for the administration said that the president was taking the time to meet with a wide variety of professionals and lay persons on both sides of the issue.

Finally, on August 9, 2001, the president announced his position in a nationally televised prime time address. He said that sixty-four stem cell lines, derived from excess embryos created in fertility clinics before nine P.M. that day, would be made available to researchers with funding from the NIH.

The new policy received decidedly mixed reviews. The far right chastised Bush for permitting any embryonic stem cell research, even using embryos that had already been destroyed. Conservatives generally agreed that Bush had given scientists plenty to work with and were reluctantly amenable, as long as there would be no more government-sanctioned destruction of "life." The consensus among both Democratic and Republican moderates was that the president had opened a door; the question was, had he opened it too much or not far enough? Many scientists were far more skeptical, especially when additional details emerged: the great majority of the lines either were owned by foreign countries such as India, Australia, and Singapore, or had already been patented by pharmaceuticals and biotechs. They questioned what it would cost to obtain approved cell lines and were concerned that the lines would have no therapeutic value. Most of them had been created by combining human cells with mouse feeder cells. The contamination by cells from another species might prevent FDA approval for clinical trials. Dr. Oswald Steward, director of the Reeve Irvine Research Center at the University of California at Irvine, was the first American scientist to obtain one of the lines in a show of good faith. His laboratory signed a contract with Geron, Inc., a pharmaceutical company based in Menlo Park, California. The line was given to Dr. Steward and his team of forty-three researchers dedicated to spinal cord repair, with the understanding that Geron would retain the rights to the commercialization of any FDA-approved technology that emerged from the Irvine lab. The first experiments were conducted in February 2002: paralyzed rats in the acute phase of injury were injected with the human stem cells. They all survived, but the extent of their recovery is being kept secret pending publication in a scientific journal. The next experiments were performed in April using the same technique on rats that had been injured for three or four months, in order to simulate the chronic phase of injury in humans. Those results were also withheld from the media pending peer-reviewed publication.

My reaction to the president's decision on August 9 was that he had created a research project—something to keep scientists busy for a while without causing too much controversy—instead of creating a therapeutic project that would lead to human trials as quickly as possible. Many scientists and disease groups hope that, given his overwhelming popularity, he will decide it is politically safe to revisit the issue.

But because the current policy means that laboratories will not receive government funding to harvest excess embryos (which would have been allowed under the Clinton guidelines), scientists have had to find other ways to make progress. The most promising development is *somatic cell nuclear transfer*, also known as nucleus

transplantation or therapeutic cloning. This is therapeutic technology that does not require the destruction
of a fertilized embryo that could be implanted in a
womb and become a human being. Instead, scientists
remove the nucleus from an unfertilized egg and replace it with the patient's DNA. Within a few days, stem
cells that will probably not face rejection by the patient's immune system can be extracted and multiplied
indefinitely. Given that we have always understood
"life" to be the creation of a union of male and female, I
can understand the moral dilemma of destroying fertilized embryos for research. But to insist that an unfertilized egg—which is actually just a cluster of cells—should
have the same standing and be entitled to the same
protections as a human being is beyond my compre-
hension.

In August 2001 the House of Representatives
banned both therapeutic cloning and reproductive
cloning (which produced Dolly the sheep) by a one-
hundred-vote margin. Senator Sam Brownback (R-
Kansas) introduced a Senate version of the bill that
would not only ban all cloning, but actually criminalize
it. Thus a spinal cord patient could travel to England for
therapy, then return to the United States, *walk* off the
airplane, and be arrested on the spot. Senators Edward

Kennedy and Dianne Feinstein countered with a far more rational bill, S.1758, which would criminalize reproductive cloning but allow therapeutic cloning to proceed, funded and regulated by the NIH. In March 2002 I testified before the Senate Health, Education, Labor, and Pensions Committee, stating in part:

> Any powerful new technology comes with the potential for abuse. But when we decide that the benefit to society is worth the risk, we take every possible precaution and go forward. The unfertilized eggs that will be used for nucleus transplantation (aka therapeutic cloning) will never leave the laboratory and will never be implanted in a womb. But if we don't make this research legal, if we don't use government funding and oversight, it will happen privately, dangerously unregulated and uncontrolled.
>
> Our country is about to lose its preeminence in science and medicine. We took a giant step backwards in the 1970s when the NIH was not allowed to fund in vitro research until an advisory commission could be formed to consider the issue. In the meantime there was rapid progress in England and the first "test tube baby" was born in 1978. For purely political reasons we did not suc-

ceed until 1981. Now IV clinics are commonplace; so far 177,000 children have been conceived in 400 facilities around the country.

Today human trials using cloned human embryos to defeat Parkinson's are under way in Sweden. In Israel macrophages, scavenger cells that eat debris in the body, are being used to repair the damaged spinal cord within two weeks of injury. The first human subject was a nineteen-year-old girl from Colorado. Last week the House of Lords in the UK passed legislation permitting research on cloned human embryos for the second time.

Those are not rogue nations behaving irresponsibly. They are allies, no less moral than we are. If we act now, we still have a chance to catch up. I urge the Senate to defeat Senator Brownback's bill S.1899 and pass S.1758.

When I started out as a patient advocate, I thought the major obstacles to achieving a cure for spinal cord injury would be a lack of funding and a shortage of scientists willing to dedicate their careers to an orphan condition. As it turned out, those would not be the problems. NIH × 2 actually succeeded: in 1998 the NIH research budget was $12 billion, but the budget for FY 2003 is just over $27.2 billion. Today regenerative medicine is attracting thousands of young postdocs all over the world who believe that effective therapies for Parkinson's, Alzheimer's, brain injury, stroke, MS, ALS, and other disorders of the central nervous system can be achieved. Instead, the main obstacle is the controversy over embryonic stem cells and therapeutic cloning. The NIH has not been allowed to fund a single grant for embryonic stem cell research using excess embryos from IVF clinics. Because of the questionable viability of the stem cell lines approved by President Bush, for many months the NIH received an alarmingly low number of grant applications, even though Health and Human Services secretary Tommy Thompson stated that some $15 million was available. By May 2002 the restrictions had eased considerably. An additional seventeen lines had been created without mouse feeder cells and the number of grant applications increased dramatically, even though the issue of therapeutic cloning remained unresolved.

I've often talked about the transition I have to make almost every morning: I have to emerge from the dreams in which I'm completely healthy and able to do anything and adjust to the reality of paralysis. In the weeks and months after my injury, that transition was often very difficult. After a few years it became less so, because I believed that the scientists were progressing well, that more funding would become available, and that the light at the end of the tunnel would continue to shine brighter every day. I never imagined for a moment that a heated political debate over a clump of cells would have such an effect on me. Now instead of waking up just to rediscover that I'm paralyzed, I wake up shocked by the realization that I may remain paralyzed for a very long time, if not forever.

Once that moment passes, I begin my day. Rationality and hope return. I'm able to focus on what can be accomplished: through education, we can change people's minds, even reverse the positions of powerful political opponents. I remember that, like it or not, my role as an advocate is to speak on behalf of other patients who will never be heard.

It is impossible to legislate compassion, yet that is what is needed most. The majority of legislators who support the most progressive research have an emotional connection to the issue—a parent with Parkinson's, a spouse with Alzheimer's, or a child with juvenile diabetes. Now we have to reach out to influential leaders in both the public and private sectors who are not directly affected by disease or disability. We have to ask them to do something much more difficult, but something that will make all the difference: just imagine what it is like to be somebody else.

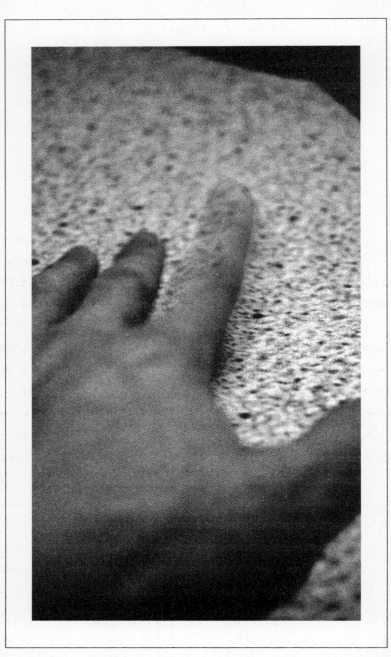

Recovery

===

In 1913, the great Spanish neuroscientist Santiago Ramón y Cajal concluded a treatise entitled *Degeneration and Regeneration of the Nervous System* by declaring, "In adult centers the nerve paths are something fixed, ended, immutable. Everything may die, nothing may be regenerated."

In the October 1998 issue of *Brainwork*, a leading journal of neuroscience, researchers stated, "In spinal cord injury, fatalism is finished, replaced by the certainty that scientists will find ways to help spinal cord victims recover."

It began with the index finger of my left hand. I was sitting in my office talking to Dana late one afternoon in November 2000. I forget the topic of our conversation, but I must have been saying something emphatically because my fingers were moving on the armrest as I spoke. Dana noticed and asked me if I was doing it on purpose. I told her that I wasn't, and she said, "Well, try."

I think if anyone else had asked me to try to move a finger nearly five years after my injury, I would have resisted. I don't like to fail. The enervation necessary to move the fingers comes from a segment of the spinal cord (T-1) far below the level of my injury. There was no reason to expect that signals from my brain could make their way down the cord and cause a finger to move. But Dana wasn't putting me on the spot; it was just a game, and it didn't matter if I lost.

I looked at the index finger of my left hand for quite a long time, literally trying to establish a relationship with it. I believe that the body wants to be whole, and I remembered the process of healing my infected left ankle several years earlier. Dana waited patiently, but I got the feeling that if I didn't do something soon she would go into the kitchen to start dinner. Staring even more intently at my finger, I suddenly said, "Move!" And it did. From the tip to the first joint, it moved up and down, tapping rhythmically on the armrest. We both watched in disbelief as it kept going. After a few moments I focused again and commanded, "Stop!" It did.

Dana leapt out of her chair and came over for a closer look. We both knew I had to do it again, perhaps several times, to prove it wasn't just a fluke. The second time, I gave the same instructions and got the same results. The third time, Dana told the finger when to move and when to stop. The fourth time, Dana gave the orders while I kept my eyes shut. It worked again.

She held me for a long moment, and when she pulled away her eyes were moist. We called up Dolly Arro, our head nurse, from her station downstairs to see if I could repeat the demonstration for her. To put it mildly, Dolly flipped out. She kept saying, "No way, no way! I have to call Harlan" (Dr. Harlan Weinberg, the

doctor in charge of my case). I turned to Dana and said,
"At least it's good for a party trick."

I had to say that in order to keep everything in perspective. I had been exercising on a regular basis since
my days as an inpatient at Kessler in the second half of
1995. By early July the bone graft from my hip to the injury site at C–2 and the titanium reinforcement wired to
the base of my skull had fully stabilized my neck. My
physical therapist, Erica Druin, started our sessions by
transferring me out of my chair onto a huge table in the
gym. I lay flat on my back on a thick mattress with my
head propped up on triangular pillows. As soon as I was
comfortable, Erica would take the pillows away and in-
struct me to move my head as far as possible from side to
side. At first I could move it about 45 degrees to the right,
but only about 30 degrees to the left because the tendon
on the right side of my neck is shorter than the other—
Dr. Jane had had to cut it to gain access to the cord. While
that movement may not sound like much, it was a sign
of real progress: I no longer had to wear the dreaded cervical collar and was actually being challenged to turn my
head with maximum effort. We always did at least three
sets of twenty repetitions of the side–to–side motion,
adding more when I wasn't too tired. Then we introduced sets of raising my head off the mattress and easing
it down again. At first I could only muster the strength to

lift my head up a few inches. But before long, with Erica's encouragement, I could raise it high enough to see my feet and hold it in that position for a very painful but highly satisfying thirty seconds. With daily repetition my neck regained lost muscle mass and flexibility.

We moved on to shoulders. I was already able to move them a little when I arrived at Kessler. Erica worked with me, both in the chair and on the mat table, by pushing my shoulders down and then applying resistance as I strained to lift them up again. The left side was decidedly weaker than the right, so she moved our sessions to the biofeedback department. I parked my chair in front of a computer screen; electrodes placed on the trapezius muscles of the shoulders provided a real-time readout in the form of a graph as I exercised. The right shoulder excursion was about 50 percent of normal, but the movement of the left peaked at a pitiful 10 to 15 percent. I told Erica that was unacceptable, which played right into her approach to my physical therapy: show a Type A personality a display of his achievement (or lack thereof) and you can harness his competitive nature to motivate improvement. The theory behind the motor deficit on the left side was that I had a case of Brown–Séquard syndrome, a common outcome of spinal cord injury, which causes greater functional recovery on one side of the body and greater sensory recovery on the other. Erica and I had decided to ignore that diagnosis, just as I had decided to ignore the opinion of experts who declared that I would never regain any functional or sensory recovery whatsoever. During the ensuing months at Kessler I spent hours in front of that screen working on my left shoulder. By the time I was discharged in December the right was up to 60 percent of normal and its weaker brother had improved to 40 percent.

Considering that only a few individuals with injuries just centimeters below the brain stem live long enough to go to a rehab center, I'm extremely grateful that I ended up in the hands of Erica and Dr. Kirshblum. Instead of relegating me to the ranks of hopeless cases, they optimized my care, using me as a test case to see what a C-2 vent–dependent quadriplegic could accomplish. They continued to work on strength and mobility in my neck and shoulders, but soon added proactive therapies usually reserved for patients with lower-level injuries.

The first was functional electrical stimulation (FES). Its purpose is to prevent muscle atrophy and to maintain good circulation. In 1995 FES was still considered experimental, even though there was no danger to the patient and the benefits seemed to be more than obvious. The technology is simple: electrodes are placed on targeted muscle groups with wires that connect to a box, about the size of a laptop, called the E–Stim. The therapist sets the electrical stimulation parameters based on the patient's size and physical condition. The electrodes are rotated every session, just as an athlete rotates exercises in the gym. All that was available at Kessler was a pair of pants with the electrodes sewn in, so I was only able to stim my legs once or twice a week. It was fairly primitive by contemporary standards, but it was a good start.

The next proactive therapies introduced in rehab were a stationary FES bicycle and a tilt table. For the FES bike, I wore a pair of shorts and individual electrodes were placed on the quadriceps and hamstrings. The current from the E–Stim machine caused those muscles to fire, enabling the legs to push the pedals of the bike. In the early sessions I could only reach the desired goal of 45 rpm for a few minutes. Eventually I was able to keep up that pace for thirty minutes nonstop, which gave me the added benefit of a good cardiovascular workout; usually my heart rate would increase by as much as forty beats per minute.

The tilt table is for weight bearing and maintaining bone density. Patients are transferred from their wheel-chairs onto a special table while it is in a horizontal po-sition and secured with straps around the knees, waist, and chest. Then the table is manually cranked up according to the patient's level of tolerance. (It requires many attempts to achieve the full upright position because the transition from lying flat to standing causes a rapid drop in blood pressure.) Putting a C-2 quadriplegic on a tilt table with the goal of having his entire weight supported by his legs and feet is extremely proactive.

The tilt table experience gave me a tremendous psychological boost. It meant that Erica as a therapist and Kessler as an institution believed it was worth preparing me for the possibility of walking again someday. After three weeks of trying, I was able to stand at 90 degrees. For the first time since my injury, I was six foot four again. Dana used to stand on the footrest of the table and lean against me with her head on my shoulder, just like the old days.

Unfortunately for most patients, the end of rehab means the end of therapy. Tilt tables, FES bikes, and E-Stim are all extremely expensive because the market for them is relatively small. Insurance companies won't pay for the patient to use them at home and they usually won't reimburse rehab facilities that would like to use them for outpatients. I was extremely fortunate to be able to purchase some of that equipment, and some of it was donated by the manufacturers. Even as I turned my attention to directing (*In the Gloaming*, 1996–97), act-ing (*Rear Window*, 1998), writing (*Still Me*, 1997–98), and advocacy (endless), I was able to maintain a regimen of exercise at the same time.

Except for the movement of my neck and shoul-ders, which is entirely voluntary (because the ener-vation is above the level of my injury), any other movement has been involuntary, requiring mechanical or electrical assistance. That's why the discovery that I could move my left index finger on command was such a momentous event.

In late November 2000 I traveled to New Orleans to give the keynote speech at the annual Symposium of Neuroscientists. Among those in attendance was Dr. John McDonald. At the time he had recently completed his postdoctoral studies in St. Louis with Dennis Choi, M.D., Ph.D., one of the world's leading researchers and one of the nine members of the consortium funded by the Christopher Reeve Paralysis Foundation. His origi-nal plan after graduating from medical school was to become a neuroscientist specializing in strokes. Appar-ently my injury caused him to choose a different path. We had met in the spring of 1999, when I spoke at a fund-raiser for the Barnes Jewish Hospital in St. Louis. Although he was only thirty-four years old, slightly stocky, with a boyish face and a carefully coiffed hair-

style reminiscent of early Robert Redford, it was immediately apparent that Dr. McDonald had acquired a vast
knowledge of the spinal cord in a short period of time.

He came into the room set aside for me as I was
preparing to join the neuroscientists at the obligatory
cocktail party. We chatted for a few moments and then
he asked me if there was anything new. I told him that
I was doing pretty well, that I didn't have any infections
at the moment, and that I was breathing without the
ventilator for longer periods of time. Then I told him
there was one specific improvement that he might find
interesting and showed him the voluntary movement
of my finger.

I don't think he would have been more astonished if
I had just walked on water. It took him a moment to recover, but when he did he practically ordered me to perform the movement inside an MRI. The purpose would
be to establish which part of my brain was sending signals down the cord, out into the peripheral nervous system and into a small subset of muscles in my left hand.
Diana De Rosa, our coordinator of travel and logistics, reminded me that I was scheduled to appear at another
fund-raiser in St. Louis on November 19. I was supposed
to fly home the next morning, but there was no reason
not to postpone the departure if the MRI at Washington
University was available. Dr. McDonald said that it would

be, even if he had to drag another patient out of it by the heels.

And so began an extraordinary collaboration that continues to this day. I gave my speech on Sunday night and was over at the MRI facility by eleven o'clock on Monday. There I was introduced to Dr. Maurizio Corbetta, assistant professor of anatomy and neurology at Washington University, trained in Milan but establishing his career in the United States. A contemporary of John's, he was already a recognized expert in MRI radiology at the time of our first meeting. After the introductions to his associates and staff, he pulled up a chair and told me what would happen in the MRI. First they would map my brain at rest; then they would ask me to move my tongue from side to side on command; finally I would see a flashing green light, the signal to move my finger as much as I could. He asked to see what that would look like, so I performed my "party trick" once again. As soon as he saw the finger move he hurried out of the room with his whole team in hot pursuit.

I found out later that Dr. Corbetta was so skeptical about voluntary movement that he hadn't even bothered to turn on the MRI before I arrived. The instructions were actually a test to see whether it was worth the time and expense of firing up the equipment. Just as there was virtually no information in the *Spinal Cord*

Manual for patients with injuries above C–4, there was apparently no precedent for recovery of function five years after the initial trauma. The common wisdom was that whatever recovery was possible would occur within the first six months, although there were several isolated cases of limited additional recovery two years postinjury. Five years was simply out of the question.

The MRI session lasted a little more than three hours. At the time I thought my greatest accomplishment was that I didn't have to be sedated. (In 1995 I made many trips down that long, claustrophobic tunnel; my greatest anxiety was air hunger, because the hose connecting me to the ventilator had to be lengthened by as much as fifteen feet. Usually I needed supplemental oxygen and tranquilizers.) The reason for the tongue movement was to map normal brain activity above the level of the injury, which could then be compared to the brain activity triggering motion far below it.

While we waited for the results, John and his assistant Linda Schultz came back to the hotel with me, Dolly, Diana, and our aide, Chris Fantini, for an early dinner. I thought I was done for the day, but John had other ideas. As I tipped back in my chair to relax, he came over and said, "Let's see you move your other fingers." I decided that my thumb might be the most likely candidate so I focused all my attention on it, trying to make the same connection that I had established with my index finger. After a few moments of concentration I silently ordered my thumb to move. It did. First there was a flicker, and then with repetition the movement became increasingly obvious. John asked me to move the thumb and forefinger simultaneously. Both digits immediately did as they were told. (A quick thought flashed across my mind—was this happening because I had been an actor for twenty-eight years and now it was "showtime"?)

John asked me to move the other fingers of my left hand, first in order and then randomly in rapid succession. I have no idea how or why they all responded. But considering the fact that none of them (except the forefinger) had moved voluntarily in more than five years, they put on quite a show. Now that we were on a roll John asked me to move the fingers of my right hand. The result? Complete failure. Not one of them would budge. Feeling my frustration, he told me to forget about it and raise my whole hand instead. (Only John MacDonald would choose that moment to move on to a much more difficult task.) He supported my arm above the armrest of my chair and let the wrist relax with the fingers pointing downward. On his command I tried to lift my right hand, something I had never even considered attempting before that moment. I could feel my whole arm tightening inside and a burning sensation from the shoulder down as I strained to make my hand move. My mind wandered back to my weight training for *Superman*, when I could bench-press more than my own weight. Now I was using the same amount of effort to pick up my wrist. How pathetic. I told myself that wasn't fair—everything's relative. Back to work. Nothing is impossible. No reason why my hand should come up, but no reason why it shouldn't, either.

The others came over to cheer me on. Now I had an audience, which was probably just what I needed. I gave it everything I had. My fingers started twitching, which meant that signals from the brain were getting through. Then, in agonizing slow motion, my wrist started to move and the hand rose up. It stopped in the level position (which I thought was amazing) but the crowd wanted more. John and Linda encouraged me; Diana, Dolly, and Chris resorted to threats, the worst being no dinner and a labor strike, which would mean spending the night sleeping in my wheelchair. That did it. I was laughing and struggling at the same time, but I finally managed to bend my wrist and raise my right hand all the way up.

Then, as we were eating dinner and I was indulging in a celebratory glass of red wine, the phone rang. It was Dr. Corbetta reporting on the preliminary results from the MRI: the electrical impulses commanding both the tongue movement and the finger movement came from the correct part of the motor cortex in the brain. This finding was also completely unexpected, because the conventional wisdom was that after a severe trauma to the central nervous system the brain would have to find alternate ways to communicate with the body below the level of injury. Many spinal cord patients have had the frustrating experience of wanting to move a leg, but getting shoulder movement instead. Often it takes months and even years of rehab to learn to compensate for the brain's tendency to give inappropriate commands after injury. An appropriate cause–and–effect relationship between the motor cortex and a targeted movement was decidedly "out of the box."

Because there had been no medical intervention, Dr. McDonald put forward the theory that the new movements were the result of regular physical exercise. Perhaps "activity–dependent training," the official term for my workout regimen, had awakened dormant pathways in the spinal cord or caused some small amount of regeneration. We agreed to undertake an official study with a patient population of one. My job was to maintain and document regular exercise; his was to quantify and verify my progress using accepted scientific methods.

On December 10, John and Linda traveled to our home in Westchester County, north of New York City. The first order of business was a complete ASIA examination, conducted at my bedside. This is a test, devised by the American Spinal Cord Injury Association, used by physicians to assess sensation and motor function. The sensory testing is done with a Q-tip and a safety pin. The patient is asked to close his eyes and feel the soft brush of the Q-tip on his face. With that sensation established as 100 percent normal, the physician moves down the body and applies the same gentle touch at random. The patient is asked to describe exactly where the Q-tip is and give a percentage score in comparison to the sensation on his face. Each answer is graded from 0 to 5, with 5 representing full sensation and accuracy of location. The safety pin is applied in the same way, but the test is even more difficult because the examiner uses both the sharp and dull ends and the patient is asked to discern the difference.

The motor function test is another head-to-toe assessment with the patient still in bed. There is a checklist of prescribed voluntary movements, measurements of the effort required to move parts of the body against resistance, and an evaluation of synapse time—the time it takes to initiate movement when the patient says "Go."

After we finished the official ASIA exam, John handed the forms to Linda and took out his video recorder. He wanted me to repeat the movements I had demonstrated in St. Louis a mere three weeks earlier. This time I was ahead of him. Expecting that he would want to see improvement, even in such a short time, I had been practicing almost daily. Under the scrutiny of the video recorder's blinking red eye, I moved the thumb and index finger of my left hand. This time the movements were greater and I could initiate them much faster. I was able to raise my right hand as before, but now I could flex it in one smooth motion that took less than ten seconds. When John or Dolly pressed a hand against the ball of my left foot, I could push it away. I was able to move individual toes on both feet. I hadn't worked on my toes before, so I was thrilled to meet the challenge of this surprise request. The most impressive movement, according to John, was a demonstration of sphincter control—not normally something I would brag about, but extremely significant in my condition because the enervation comes from the lowest segment of the spinal cord. If you can contract the sphincter on command it positively proves that there are intact, functioning pathways all the way from the brain to the bottom of the cord.

The ASIA scale ranges from *A* to *E*: *A* represents virtually no movement or sensation, while *E* is the classification for a score of 100 percent in both areas. My first ASIA exam was conducted at Kessler on July 5 and 6, 1995. In the categories of Motor Function, Light Touch, and Pin Prick, I scored 2 percent, 8 percent, and 6 percent, respectively, which made me an ASIA *A*. Now, on the ASIA exam conducted by John McDonald six and a half years later, I scored 10 percent on Motor Function, an incredible 56 percent on Light Touch, and a significant improvement on Pin Prick, up to 22 percent.

John used every superlative in the book when he showed me the scores. He was the proverbial kid in a candy store, a four-year-old on Christmas morning. I appreciated his enthusiasm and was gratified to learn that my daily regimen had been worthwhile. He left on cloud nine, but I was left to face the reality that nothing in my everyday life had changed. I had graduated to ASIA *B*, but I was still in the same chair, still on the same vent, still requiring professional care 24/7. I took some consolation in the fact that I was recovering and that I had just scored a major upset in the world of science and medicine. At the same time I felt bad for people with degenerative diseases such as ALS, multiple sclerosis, and muscular dystrophy. What could exercise do for them? Just like victims of Parkinson's, Alzheimer's, diabetes, and so many other diseases, they need scientific research as much as I do. We discussed our priorities internally at the CRPF and decided that funding cutting–edge research would remain our primary mission; at the same time we voted to allocate more money for quality–of–life grants. On May 3, 2002, we opened the Christopher and Dana Reeve Paralysis Resource Center to provide critical information and support for victims and their families suddenly facing paralysis.

I followed Dr. McDonald's instructions to keep exercising and trying to make my body move. The exercise was carefully regulated, but it was left up to me to experiment with movement. John's advice was to try anything, because that was the only way to find out which pathways were still intact and to see if others could be reawakened. Fortunately Chris Fantini had just completed his training and was now a licensed physical therapist. We worked together to create a protocol that would test enervation and muscle strength in every area.

Because I had spent years riding the FES bicycle on a fairly regular basis, we decided to see if I could create spontaneous movement in either leg. As I lay flat Chris would place my foot on his right shoulder and then push my leg forward until it was bent 90 degrees at the knee. I would say "go" to let him know that my brain was issuing a command, and then push as hard as I could to straighten out the leg. The first few times nothing happened. Saying "go" to my leg was about as productive as saying "drop" to Chamois when she fetched a tennis ball. Repetition was the key: during the fourth or fifth attempt I could see the quads in my right leg start to flicker and Chris could feel my foot pushing against his shoulder. Soon the left leg followed suit and Chris had to lean against my feet, providing resistance to make the exercise more difficult as the movements grew stronger.

Building on my ability to flex my right wrist, we moved on to the forearm. Chris or one of the other aides who had been taught the routines placed my forearm across my chest, supporting the weight of the arm with an open palm under the elbow. The task was to fully extend the forearm, using my triceps and forearm extensors. Strength was not an issue, thanks again to regular E–Stim of my arms over a long period of time. The challenge was to establish the same connection that made it possible to move one finger with signals originating from the correct part of the motor cortex. As I began to experiment with movement, the problem was overflow: muscles would fire in irrelevant areas. Biceps and deltoids might kick in when I only wanted activation in the triceps. But I knew that overflow could be controlled with practice; it was a much more tractable condition than minimal movement or none at all.

Forearm extension from placement across the chest was a routine maneuver in the range-of-motion protocol dating back to rehab in 1995. My body and mind were well accustomed to somebody else moving my arm for me. Now we were attempting to harness strength, habit, and willpower to move it on my own. It only took about a week to discover that when I sharpened my mental focus—in this case trying to concentrate only on my triceps—the overflow subsided. Now I was able to extend the forearm, tenuously at first, but then with more speed and assurance. Within a month the synapse time to initiate movement in both forearms and both legs was practically instantaneous—a sure sign that just like the index finger, the signals were coming from the correct part of the motor cortex.

By January 2001, I was spending as much as three to four hours a day on physical therapy. We would work the lower body one day, the upper body the next, combining E-Stim, the FES bike, and voluntary motion against resistance. The forearm extensions had led to gaining the ability to fully extend both arms and raise them up like wings. Then I learned to start with my arms fully opened horizontally and bring them down to rest at my side. I could do this one at a time or simultaneously, with an aide giving light support at the wrists and elbows.

One day I decided to see if I could sit up by myself out of the wheelchair. Again, there was no reason to assume I could do that, but no reason to assume I couldn't. (I had been using the E-Stim on my abdominal and paraspinal muscles as part of my regular routine.) Dolly and Chris positioned the chair next to the tilt table and transferred me onto the edge. Chris stood behind the table in case I fell backward, while Dolly covered the front. I asked her to plant my feet the width of my shoulders to give me a base of support, and I asked Chris to pull my upper body fully upright, making sure that I wasn't leaning left or right. Then I asked them both to let go. Nothing happened, which (for once) was exactly the desired outcome. I just sat there. All the other exercises required strenuous effort; sitting upright on my own required me to relax and allow the continuous, subtle interactions of nerves and muscles to create balance. When I started to fade to the right or the left, I commanded the muscles on the opposing side to compensate and bring me back to center. I was overjoyed to find that sitting on my own wasn't very difficult. I reflected on the fact that balance is natural, it's where the body wants to be. Maybe after all these years it still remembers. That's why practically anybody can get on a bicycle after twenty years and pedal away.

I closed my eyes, just as an experiment. I didn't know if visual reference was necessary to keep me upright. Once again, nothing happened. For nearly five minutes I remained motionless, and then I started to slump forward as fatigue set in. My head, which weighs about twenty-six pounds, was the first to go and then my upper body followed. But I had been sitting virtually untouched for more than half an hour.

Today I look back at that experience as one of the three most significant milestones in my history as a spinal cord patient. The first was discovering that my injury was not complete; the second was finding out that I could breathe on my own, if only for short periods of time. The ability to initiate movement far below the level of my injury and simply to sit with little or no assistance meant there was even more reason to hope.

I went back to St. Louis in February for another round of testing and evaluation. The functional MRI showed that all the movements I had acquired since the last visit were also being directed by the correct part of the motor cortex, with some recruitment from the opposite hemisphere of the brain. The ASIA exam was a great success: because my motor and sensory scores had improved dramatically, I was reclassified as an ASIA C. Dr. McDonald was again ecstatic, describing these results as "history in the making." I was encouraged by the thought that since my improvement was the result of exercise, it might translate into insurance companies paying for equipment that could help other patients recover enough function to return to work or school. Wouldn't it be more profitable to give patients who meet certain criteria the tools and training they need to get better and go away?

Proof of that principle had already been convincingly demonstrated by Dr. Reggie Edgerton at UCLA. Guided by the theory that it doesn't take much brain activity to walk, he experimented with paraplegics who had control of their upper body but were paralyzed from the waist down. He placed these patients on a treadmill, flipped the switch, and their legs responded as the machine went into motion. At first they needed the assistance of several physical therapists to place the feet correctly and to avoid sprained or broken ankles. Gradually Dr. Edgerton and his team found that if the average patient stepped on the treadmill an hour a day for approximately sixty days, he or she would then be able to walk over ground on their own assisted only by a cane. When I visited his lab I saw an eighteen–year–old paraplegic who had completed the training get out of a chair by himself, walk quite normally across the room, sit down in another chair, then get up again, still completely unassisted, and walk back to his original seat. Technically speaking he was not cured, but because of this specialized activity–dependent training, he had achieved extraordinary functional recovery. He is no longer a burden to his insurance company. In my case it was obvious that hard exercise was keeping me out of the hospital, but I still wondered how and when it would significantly change my life.

I returned home and intensified my workouts. I rode for longer periods of time on the bike, increased the repetitions of my voluntary movements, and raised the voltage on the E–Stim machine. I put more time and effort into breathing on my own, trying to develop enough strength in my diaphragm to eventually wean myself off the ventilator. Professors Daniel Martin and Paul Davenport from the University of Florida at Gainesville introduced a novel theory. During exercise, carbon dioxide builds up in the body. That triggers a demand for more oxygen, and the average person responds by breathing faster. Their approach (which they had successfully demonstrated in rats) is to *reduce* the amount of air pumped into the patient by the ventilator during exercise and let the level of CO_2 rise as high as the patient can tolerate. With enough repetition, as the patient is suffering the equivalent of pulling six g's in a jet fighter, the brain stem should get the message and kick-start autonomic breathing. The normal range of CO_2 in the bloodstream of a person at rest is anywhere between 35 and 45 percent. When I started using their weaning method my CO_2 was a feeble 25 percent. By May 2002 my resting percentage was up to 34 percent, and when I was on the bike I could endure levels of 47 to 49 percent for as long as forty-five minutes. Autonomic breathing hasn't happened yet, but I'm still trying.

July 8, 2001, was another watershed moment—literally. I was in St. Louis again for more testing and John decided it was time to throw me in the pool. Of course he didn't actually throw me, but it was an "out of the box" experience both for me and for his staff of physical therapists. No patient had ever gone into the pool while attached to a ventilator. Most rehab facilities wouldn't even consider aquatherapy for a vent-dependent quadriplegic. What if water gets into the hose? What if the ventilator falls into the pool? John's answer: somebody with an IQ above double digits holds on to the vent, and two or three others keep the hose out of the water.

Soon I was floating on my back for the first time in six years, with just a collar around my neck and an inflatable belt around my waist. I relaxed completely and reveled in the sensation of the warm water all around me. A therapist held my shoulders and gently made my body "snake" from side to side. I watched my feet, which now seemed far away, swishing back and forth. I had the sense that my body was actually lengthening as the vertebrae were relieved of the compression they have to withstand when I sit in my wheelchair.

After ten minutes of sheer bliss they put me to work. I had to perform every movement I could do on land, and then some. Suddenly a therapist said, "How about standing?" I could tell that the only acceptable answer was "Sure." The next moment many hands were holding me upright. Someone put rubber boots on my feet and secured five-pound weights around my ankles. I was asked to bend my knees and let my body down until the water level was just below my trachea. The next move would be to push with my legs and stand. I focused on my quads, once again making the connection that had by now become an integral part of my life. When I was ready I gave myself a silent "Go." The muscles fired and I shot straight up. Suddenly I was towering above everyone around me. John, Linda, Dolly, a documentary film crew, and various onlookers applauded and cheered as if they were watching a moon launch.

But there was more to come. Now that I was standing, of course the next thing to do was walk. I had taken
steps on Dr. Edgerton's treadmill before, but there my
body was suspended by a harness and the motion of
the treadmill made my legs move. This was completely
different. For the first time I was actually being asked to
initiate walking on my own.

The helping hands still held me upright. As I shifted
my entire weight onto my right leg a therapist told me
to look at my left foot and kick it forward. That was not
much different from pushing my leg forward, which I
had done hundreds of times against Chris Fantini's
shoulder. I kicked hard from my left knee and suddenly
saw that my left foot was now ahead of me, a few inches
above the bottom of the pool. Another therapist told
me to push off my right leg and transfer my weight to
the left. It worked. (One small step for man, et cetera . . .)
Then we repeated the process, kicking the right foot forward and shifting weight to take another step. In that
first attempt I took eight steps before I reached the end
of the hose and had to be floated back to home base. As
we continued my body seemed to remember what to
do. The leg thrust and weight transfer became easier
and looked more normal. By the end of the session I
had walked in water eight times.

By September 2001 my exercise program included weekly aquatherapy at the Gaylord rehab facility in nearby Connecticut. The first six sessions were supervised by their physical therapists and then I was allowed to use the pool with two nurses and two aides from our team. The two hours set aside for me on Friday afternoons soon became a precious reward, an eagerly anticipated treat at the end of the week. We don't have enough people to help me walk, but we still do most of the other exercises. Some days are better than others, usually depending on how well I sleep the night before, but the overall progress has been extremely gratifying.

The payoff came on January 20, 2002, when I traveled to St. Louis once again for the assessment that would complete the study. The evaluation took three days. In addition to the usual physical exam, the ASIA exam, and another three-hour session in the MRI, John and his team measured all the muscle activity, including the diaphragm, with an electromyogram (EMG). I felt like a giant pincushion, but I knew that the EMG needles would give a more accurate reading of synapse time and the degree of enervation needed to create movement.

Fortunately for all concerned, I hit a home run. The Motor Function score went up from 11 to 20, Light

Touch jumped from 57 to 78, and the Pin Prick total soared to 56 from a previous high of 22. Now John had accumulated enough data to publish a scientific article demonstrating that activity–dependent training promotes functional recovery in chronic spinal cord injury. He said the test had to be so thorough and repeated over a long period of time (almost two years) because thirty neuroscientists could stand at the bedside, watch me move, and still say it wasn't happening. The article would be certain to cause controversy. We hoped it would also cause rehab facilities and neuroscientists (as well as insurance companies) to look at physical therapy in a new way. Perhaps the aggressive approach that had led to significant improvement in my case would now be used to treat not only other spinal cord patients, but victims of strokes, MS, and other central nervous system disorders as well.

Faith

Universalists believe that God is too good to damn people, and the Unitarians believe that people are too good to be damned by God.... Universalists believe in a God who embraces everyone, and this is central to their belief that lasting truth is found in all religions, and that dignity and worth is innate to all people regardless of sex, color, race, or class.

—*Minister Thomas Starr King, c. 1800*

... And we are willing to make public, as part of our religious practice, what we believe—that the human family is one, and that the love that binds us is greater than the fears that divide us.

—*Barbara J. Pescan*

After my encounter with Scientology I moved on in my search to discover the relevance of spirituality. But during the next twenty years, culminating with my injury in 1995, I tended to focus on the Big Questions only when I was not preoccupied with activities and issues of the moment. Others tried to impose their beliefs on me: the Scientologists begged me to return, and my acting coach in the eighties wanted me to become a follower of the Buddhist leader Baba Muktananda. During the Superman years I received hundreds of letters from fans explaining that Jor-el is God and his son Kal-el (Superman) is Christ, sent from Krypton to be raised by a humble family in Kansas before beginning his mission to save the world. I could appreciate the obvious parallel, and I did consider Superman to be a significant mythical icon in popular culture. But if religious individuals saw Superman as Christ, and identified me as Superman, then what? How did I ascend from working New York actor to present–day Messiah?

In 1987, Gae Exton and I went our separate ways. Our relationship had been tenuous for some time. I returned to New York in early February as soon as I finished filming *Superman IV*, leaving Matthew (seven) and Alexandra (three) behind. The separation was amicable and we readily agreed to put the best interests of the children above all else: joint custody, British and American citizenship, and mutual consent on all important decisions. Still, I was nearly overcome with guilt. As a child of divorce myself, I could only hope that they wouldn't have as hard a time as I did.

Now that I was living three thousand miles away, I needed to find ways to ease the pain and to remain a strong presence in their lives. In late February I hosted a documentary on the future of flight, which was filmed at the Air and Space Museum in Washington. I kept a video recorder with me and made tapes of myself next to the *Spirit of St. Louis*, at the Washington Monument and the Jefferson Memorial. I even included a drive–by glimpse of the White House. Back in New York I taped kids in the park where we had played countless games of hide–and–seek; I went to the corner deli to tape greetings from the man who used to give Matthew a banana when I got my morning coffee; from the roof of our apartment I took shots of the Museum of Natural History across the street, our second home on rainy days. At the end of the video I looked into the camera and told them we'd see each other very soon.

I did my best to sound positive and cheerful, but even as I dropped the tape off at the post office, I wasn't sure if I'd been able to mask the pain. I needed a real distraction, anything that would make me feel better. Drugs and alcohol were out of the question; I didn't want to escape reality by making myself less conscious.

Flipping through my mail as I walked back from the post office, I came across a brochure for "Loving Relationships Training." I gathered from the material that their mission was to help people find happiness by learning to love anyone and everyone we meet on life's path. Weekend seminars, open to newcomers and graduates alike, were held several times a year in cities around the world. The next one in New York was only two weeks away. I decided that was more than a coincidence; maybe I was meant to find out about this source of spiritual healing at one of the lowest points of my life.

I reserved a place and showed up at a midtown hotel on Friday afternoon to begin my weekend of LRT. At the registrar's desk I filled out forms that included complete confidentiality and handed over a check for

$1,500. Then I found myself in one of the ballrooms of the hotel, seated among three hundred others waiting patiently for the seminar to begin. I looked around and saw apparently normal people of all ages and descriptions. At least no one seemed tense or semirobotic, a marked contrast to many of the Scientologists in 1975.

Soon a side door opened and the leaders joined us—a man and a woman in their early forties, both fit and attractive in a well-tailored suit and a colorful designer dress. There were no workbooks, no videos, no E-Meters or personality tests. They simply began talking, taking turns as they addressed us. Although they must have delivered the same message many times before, they didn't sound rehearsed and I didn't feel that I was attending a lecture. They were relaxed, warm, and intimate in front of such a large gathering; if you've ever heard Deepak Chopra speak you get the idea.

They began by going into more detail about LRT as a basis for living, and then explained how we would spend much of the weekend in practical application. The premise was simple: All human beings are equal and equally worthy of loving and being loved. All our relationships must be informed by love, whether inside the family, among friends, or even in the fleeting moments as we pass others on the street. When we sit down at a restaurant, how many of us really pay attention to the waiter? We might listen for a moment while he reads the specials, but could anyone describe him accurately after dinner? The same applies to bus drivers, tollbooth collectors, all the people we scarcely notice as we follow our own pursuits. All it takes is a brief moment of eye contact, which acknowledges the equality of another human being. Even that is a loving relationship.

Like other simple equations, many people find that one almost impossible to solve. How does one become able to love a relative when there has been nothing but jealousy or hatred for years? Are we expected to love someone who has deliberately harmed us in some way? The first step, which we were asked to take on Saturday morning, was to declare a statute of limitations on damage done to us by our parents. Now we used notebooks, putting it in writing that the statute had expired. From this day forward we agreed individually and collectively to forgive any grievances still held against them. Next we made a list of all the people who immediately came to mind as enemies, detractors, rivals, and anyone we had ever envied or knowingly deceived. We were given only ten minutes to think of names and write them down, which was probably a good idea because most of us could have gone on for hours.

The next task was to list ten words that best described ourselves, not taking into account what others might think. Then we had to write down ten words defining the person we would like to be—not a role model, but the embodiment of our own potential. After that we were given a few moments to find a partner. Each pairing would remain together for the rest of the weekend. This was a scary proposition, because I have to admit I had not evolved to being nonjudgmental. Put simply, I didn't want to get stuck with some weirdo. (Actually, most people thought the weirdest thing about the weekend was that I was there in the first place.) Fortunately my radar had identified three very attractive women in the group on Friday afternoon, so I immediately made a beeline for Choice A and managed to get there before the competition. I should have made a mental note that I might not succeed with LRT: we had just spent a day and a half learning that everyone is equal and equally worthy of love, and here I was practicing basic Darwinism. We had to move quickly because there was no negotiating; once eye contact was made with one of the other 299 people in the room, that was it.

My partner was a tall, very good-looking blond woman in her early twenties. She had left her small hometown in Pennsylvania to pursue a modeling career in the Big Apple when she was only eighteen. Apparently she was successful at work but unlucky in love.

She described herself as habitually attracted to the wrong men—ones who broke promises, mistreated her and diminished her already low self-esteem. I shared with her my wish that people would stop assuming that some of us have no problems.

The one-on-one tasks continued the rest of the afternoon and most of Sunday morning. We wrote and exchanged lists of people and things we love, hate, want to remember, and would like to forget. As usual we weren't given much time, but now I found it quite exhilarating to free-associate. It was very liberating to write down the first thoughts that came into my mind and then share them, uncensored, with someone I had never met but to whom I soon felt I could say anything.

Then all three hundred of us split into groups of fifteen to twenty, including our partners, and fanned out to a number of restaurants in the area for lunch. By this time we were all on a high, having affirmed the positive and banished the negative. The waiters were literally overwhelmed with respect. We ate our food slowly, taking time to savor every bite. We listened intently as the man who was one of the two leaders of the seminar described the mind-blowing spiritual experience of Harmonic Convergence, which, according to Mayan prophecies, marked the beginning of a new age of universal peace. Then he moved on to the next step for LRT

graduates who were serious about going further: rebirthing in a hot tub. I had no idea what that meant but
I wondered where, when, and did my partner get to
come?

Sadly, at that point they lost me. Rebirthing was
conducted by two certified rebirthers working with one
LRT graduate in someone's home—presumably a re-
birther who could afford a New York apartment with a
hot tub. The theory was that when most of us were born
it was a highly traumatic experience: we emerged from
the dark comfort of the womb to be greeted by harsh
lights, frightening creatures in masks, and a sudden,
violent slap on the back. Apparently this first impres-
sion of the world is so overwhelming that we spend our
lifetime crippled by fear and anger. The sheer effort of
coping with those feelings or struggling to deny them
prevents us from becoming the free, loving, and fulfilled
people that we deserve to be. Rebirthing sessions in the
hot tub are meant first to re-create our actual experience
of being born in this lifetime. Then the student and the
rebirthers work together to replace that horrific scenario
with its exact opposite. Curled up in the fetal position in
the moments before birth, we emerge to find ourselves
immersed in soothing warm water and cradled by loving arms. The first sounds we hear are gentle music and
soft voices welcoming us into the world.

Needless to say, the three rebirthings I had were extremely pleasant, almost to the point of sensory over-
load. The problem was that it seemed obvious what was
expected of me. I tried my hardest to place myself once
again inside my mother's womb, but in spite of a long
career as an actor with a vivid imagination, I couldn't do
it. The rebirthers gave me more love and support than
any baby could ever hope for and were quite emotional
about my "breakthrough." I knew it would be downright
cruel to tell them I was faking it. They urged me to be
rebirthed at least twice a month (at $200 a pop) to reaf-
firm my innocence and to prevent negativity from
working its way back into my life. I assured them I
would give it serious thought, but after the third session
in the hot tub I never contacted them again. I thought
about staying in touch with my beautiful partner but
decided against it because rebound relationships usually don't work. For the best interests of the children, as
well as myself, at that time I needed to be alone.

The reason I disengaged from LRT was much the
same as the reason I disavowed Scientology: I don't believe in instant fixes. I don't believe we can write an affirmation to forgive our parents or others who have
wronged us and consider it done. I don't believe we can
write a new script for our lives by simulating a pleasant
birth.

I think that if we want to be true to ourselves, finding answers to the most important questions of life is a
process. The time it takes to make genuine discoveries
and find true beliefs varies with every individual. For
most of my life faith was a very difficult concept. I understood it to mean the willingness to believe in the
value of something that can't be known in advance or
even defined, but I couldn't put it into practice. I was
the customer who demands an extended warranty or a
money-back guarantee. As an actor my job was to serve
the story, and I truly enjoyed the process involved in
doing that. Many actors get tired of playing one part for
a long time; I always enjoyed long runs (such as *A Matter of Gravity*, *Fifth of July*, and *The Aspern Papers*) because
every performance was an opportunity to learn more
about the character and the intentions of the play-
wright, with a safety net of knowing the outcome in advance.

My first act of faith was not a religious one; it happened when Dana and I were married. I had always
been afraid of marriage, perhaps because there had
been a long history of failures for many generations in
my family. But on a spring day in 1992, next to a picture window overlooking the Berkshire Mountains in
Massachusetts, I repeated the vows because somehow
I absolutely believed that they were true. I couldn't

know or define our future ahead of time; I acted on faith. It was an enormous step forward.

Three years later I lost the use of almost my entire body. My identity and self-esteem had always been based in the physical world. I cherished health, athletics, travel, and adventure. At first I couldn't imagine living without those things. In an instant, paralysis created an indescribable void. Family, friends, and well-wishers from around the world assured me that prayers and my faith in God would comfort me. I tried to pray but I didn't feel any better, nor did I make any kind of connection with God. I wondered what was wrong with me: I had broken my neck and become paralyzed, possibly forever, but still hadn't found God. A close friend about my age had lived through tremendous upheavals since childhood and finally found faith. His advice to me was "Fake it till you make it." In other words, just pray and sooner or later it will have meaning. I tried and failed. Even in the sleepless predawn hours at Kessler, my mind wandered and my emotions overcame me.

Finally I decided to stop beating myself up. I wasn't in school anymore and I didn't have to get good grades in religious studies. When reporters continued to ask me about the importance of religion in my life I began to answer by saying that I'm not sure if there is a God, but I try to behave as if He is watching.

Gradually I have come to believe that spirituality is found in the way we live our daily lives. It means spending time thinking about others. It's not so hard to imagine that there is some kind of higher power. We don't have to know what form it takes or exactly where it exists; just to honor it and try to live by it is enough. Because we are human we will often fail, but at least we know that we do not deserve to be punished. That knowledge makes us safe and willing to try again.

As these thoughts unfolded in the process of learning to live my new life, I had no idea that I was becoming a Unitarian. In my late forties faith and organized religion unexpectedly converged. Dana, Will, and I attend services regularly, bringing along whichever nurse happens to be on duty. Sue Citarella, a lifelong practicing Catholic, has come with us a number of times and finds the welcoming, nonjudgmental atmosphere to be very rewarding. In the words of our minister, "We see our church as a place where people can be truly religious because they can be true to themselves, where honest doubt is not taken for heresy, and where the beliefs of the past and the present become the inspiration for future growth and discovery."

Dana and I were talking after church not too long ago, reflecting on the service and religion in general. I told her that what I liked about Unitarian Universalism is that you are not presumed guilty when you walk in the door. You don't have to confess your sins to a priest and be told that ten Hail Marys and five Our Fathers will make you square with God for at least another week. God isn't a warrior or a terrifying father figure who will embrace you in his arms but take you out to the woodshed in an instant if you misbehave. This church doesn't demand a percentage of your income in order to belong. This God understands that many of us don't know where He lives or even how to spell His name. He knows that it isn't easy for us to love ourselves, our families, or even our neighbors, let alone the rest of humanity. Instead He asks us just to do our best, trusting our innate ability to discern the truth. As Abraham Lincoln said, "When I do good I feel good. When I do bad I feel bad. And that's my religion."

In the 1960s, hippies painted their vans with the symbol for peace and the words "God Is Love." Most of them were probably thinking about sex, but in the deepest sense of the word what they wrote was actually quite profound. I think they and Honest Abe were right.

Hope

Hope is itself a species of happiness, and,
perhaps, the chief happiness which this world
affords: but, like all other pleasures
immoderately enjoyed, the excesses of
hope must be expiated by pain; and
expectations improperly indulged
must end in disappointment.

—*Samuel Johnson*

Anyone familiar with Superman knows that ever since he was created by Jerry Siegel and Joe Shuster in 1938, his purpose has always been to symbolize and uphold the values of "Truth, Justice and the American way." During the filming of the first *Superman* at Pinewood Studios in England, on the wall of his office director Richard Donner proudly displayed a model of Superman in flight. The superhero carries a banner with only one word: "Verisimilitude," which the *American Heritage Dictionary* defines as "the quality of appearing to be true or real." The challenge for the production team was to make the miniature, optical, mechanical, and flying effects absolutely convincing. Everyone involved in the film knew that the one-line tease on the advertising posters was going to be "You'll believe a man can fly." That was a very tall order given the state of film technology in 1977. The challenge for me as an actor was to equal the achievements of the technical experts; if they could create verisimilitude, then I had to do the same. The first step was to examine the values embraced by the character and passed down for generations. Truth and justice seemed relatively easy to understand, but what about "the American way"? What does that mean? Is the American way different from the way of other countries that uphold democracy and human rights? Isn't it dangerous or at least counterproductive to imply that the American way is somehow better than others?

I posed some of these questions to Dick Donner soon after I arrived in London to begin preproduction for the film. He seemed pleased by my enthusiasm and by this evidence that I was taking my job seriously, but told me to go figure it out. The first day of shooting was only three months away and he was up to his neck in technical problems. Every department seemed to need final decisions yesterday.

After considerable thought and discussion with friends, including a number of politicians who were fans of Superman, I decided that because the character is a hero for the entire world, nationalism was not an issue. When Lois Lane asks Superman, "Who are you?" he replies, "A friend." That makes him, above all else, a symbol of hope. In the face of adversity, hope often comes in the form of a friend who reaches out to us. I thought about other aspects of the American way and the basic rights of pluralistic societies: equal opportunity, equal rights, tolerance, free speech, and fair play. For centuries wars have been fought in defense of those rights. In countries where they never existed or were taken away, millions of people have risked their lives to escape. Most of them left with only a few possessions and the hope of not being turned away by a free society.

To say that I believed in Superman is quite an un-derstatement. Of course I knew it was only a movie, but it seemed to me that the values embodied by Superman on the screen should be the values that prevail in the real world.

WHEN I SUDDENLY BECAME A QUADRIPLEGIC MY DEEPEST, almost overwhelming reaction was simply "It's not fair." Intellectually, I knew that life isn't fair and that bad things can happen to any of us at any time. Emotion-ally, I couldn't control myself. I demanded an answer to the apparently unanswerable question: Why me? What did I do to deserve this? It's not fair. With time my irra-tional anger about the injustice of my injury subsided. But the experience left a residual effect that still informs the way I look at the world today: I want to see fair play.

I don't care if it's proper officiating in baseball games, how coaches make up teams in Pee Wee hockey, ethical conduct in business, or how we choose our representatives in government.

Although I am a registered Democrat, like many of my friends I vote for candidates based on the issues. Here in New York State I supported Democrats Hillary Clinton and Charles Schumer for the Senate, but voted for Republicans Rudy Giuliani and George Pataki for mayor and governor, respectively. When I joined other advocates in the early 1990s to save the National Endowment for the Arts, two of our most formidable opponents were Senators Arlen Specter (R–Pennsylvania) and Jesse Helms (R–North Carolina). Since 1997 I have worked closely with Senator Specter on health care reform, rights of the disabled, and increased funding for biomedical research. When the Senate voted on the Animal Welfare Act of 2002, Jesse Helms introduced an amendment excluding rats, mice, and birds from the protections afforded higher animals such as dogs and primates. If the Helms amendment had been defeated, researchers would have been required to conduct experiments on rats, mice, and birds under the same conditions as an operation on a human being. The expense involved would have put an end to much of the critical basic research currently under way across the country.

In my younger days I would never have imagined siding with Jesse Helms on *anything*. With time I've learned that the most effective way to change policy in Washington is to join forces with the most influential allies on a case-by-case basis.

Those examples of nonpolitical alliances are meant to give a context to the 2000 presidential election. I believe the outcome had a direct effect on the hope for a radical overhaul of the electoral process, the hope for an enlightened energy and environmental policy, and the hope for government support of the most advanced biomedical research.

Those of us who hoped for a fair debate leading to governmental approval of therapeutic cloning were extremely disturbed by a media opportunity that took place at the White House on April 10. The president urged the Senate to pass the Brownback bill, S.1899, which would ban all forms of cloning. He stated, "I believe all human cloning is wrong, and both forms of cloning ought to be banned, for the following reasons. First, anything other than a total ban on human cloning would be unethical. Research cloning would contradict the most fundamental principle of medical ethics, that no human life should be exploited or extinguished for the benefit of another."

At the president's side, in full dress uniform, was

former New York City police officer Stephen McDonald, still confined to a wheelchair sixteen years after suffering a gunshot wound that left him paralyzed from the shoulders down. Officer McDonald is a devout Catholic. When he was interviewed by the media after the president's press conference, he said that his accident was "God's will" and echoed the pope's position on the sanctity of human life.

As I watched the event live on CNN I felt great sympathy for Stephen McDonald, who took the trouble to visit me with his family soon after I was admitted to Kessler. He had many helpful things to say about living with a high cervical injury. As an anxious father particularly concerned about our youngest, Will, I was delighted to meet his son Connor, who was not yet born when his father was paralyzed. We only met for a short time, but he seemed to be a perfectly normal nine-year-old and I could sense a special bond in spite of—or perhaps because of—Stephen's disability. Patti McDonald, Stephen's wife, was a great comfort to Dana; they talked many times about the issues facing the families and caregivers of people living with disabilities. That's why it was painful for me to see him strategically placed next to the podium on television that day. I felt he was being used. Politicians do this sort of thing all the time.

Is there any elected official who hasn't been pho-
tographed reading to small children? But the issue of
therapeutic cloning was a current debate that stirred up
emotions as well as ethical, moral, religious, and political concerns. I thought the president was unduly attempting to exert his influence, especially in light of the
fact that the bioethics panel appointed to advise him
had not yet issued its opinion. Once again, what happened to fair play?

I'm certain that I was only one among many who
were greatly relieved to find an op–ed piece in *The New
York Times* on April 25 by Michael Gazzaniga, Ph.D., director of the Center for Cognitive Neuroscience at Dart-
mouth College. A fellow of the American Association for
the Advancement of Science and the American Neuro-
logical Association, he is also one of the distinguished
members of the president's advisory panel. He wrote:

> It was a surprise when, on April 10, the President
> announced his decision to ban cloning of all kinds.
> His opinions appeared fully formed even though
> our panel has yet to prepare a final report. . . .
>
> Some religious groups and ethicists argue
> that the moment of transfer of cellular material is
> an initiation of life and establishes a moral equiv-

alency between a developing group of cells and a human being. This point of view is problematic when viewed with modern biological knowledge.

We wouldn't consider this clump of cells even equivalent to an embryo formed in normal human reproduction. And we now know that in normal reproduction as many as 50 percent to 80 percent of all fertilized eggs spontaneously abort and are simply expelled from the woman's body. It is hard to believe that under any religious belief system people would grieve and hold funerals for these natural events. Yet, if these unfortunate zygotes are considered human beings, then logically people should. . . .

The biological clump of cells produced in biomedical cloning is the size of the dot on this i. It has no nervous system and is not sentient in any way. It has no trajectory to becoming a human being; it will never be implanted in a woman's uterus. What it probably does have is the potential for the cure of diseases affecting millions of people.

When I joined the panel, officially named the President's Council on Bioethics, I was confident that a sensible and a sensitive policy might evolve from what was sure to be a cacophony of voices

of scientists and philosophers representing a spectrum of opinions, beliefs and intellectual back-
grounds. I only hope that in the end the President
hears his council's full debate.

The temperature of the debate rose dramatically in
May 2002. Proponents on both sides of the Brownback
bill ran television ads in Utah, North Dakota, Georgia,
and Washington, D.C., trying to win swing votes and
threaten senators who were up for reelection. Support-
ers of S.1899 such as the Family Research Council tried
to convince the public that therapeutic cloning means
"killing babies" and the creation of "embryo farms." Opponents explained somatic cell nuclear transfer and
pleaded with the Senate, "Don't legislate away hope."

A poll taken by the highly respected firm Caravan
Inc. showed that 68 percent of the American public was
in favor of therapeutic cloning, 28 percent were opposed, and 4 percent had no opinion. Opponents of the
research who objected because of deeply held religious
or ethical convictions, who were absolutely true to their
beliefs (like Stephen McDonald), I felt had to be respected. Much more troublesome were senators like Bill
Frist (R–Tennessee), and of course Senator Brownback,
who seemed to lack a consistent point of view.

In testimony before a Senate subcommittee, Senator Brownback stated that he was in favor of in vitro fertility clinics and added, "Many of my friends have had fine children that way." Senator Harkin pointed out that during the process of creating a viable embryo for a couple that could be successfully implanted in the woman's uterus, an average of eight to ten fertilized but now unwanted embryos are routinely discarded as medical waste. Brownback replied, "I understand the majority of them are put up for adoption. But let's return to the question of cloning."

According to the 1999 Centers for Disease Control report "Assisted Reproductive Technology Success Rates," 250 babies were born to couples using five IVF clinics in Kansas that year. An estimated 6,000 eggs were retrieved and approximately 70 percent of those were successfully fertilized and developed, creating some 4,000 embryos. Consistent with the average statistics in 400 IVF clinics across the country, a third of the embryos in the Kansas clinics didn't develop enough to be useful; a third were frozen for the possible creation of a sibling; the remaining third were thrown away with the informed consent of the donors. According to Sean Tipton, director of public affairs for the American Society for Reproductive Medicine, only one of the five clinics in Kansas offers an embryo adoption program. In addition, he estimates that in the twenty-one-year history of in vitro fertilization in the United States, less than 100 families have had children through embryo donation.

If Senator Brownback doesn't know the facts, even in his own state, is he qualified to propose legislation on the issue? If he is aware that *any* leftover embryos are legally being destroyed in Kansas, how does he condone that in light of his fervent opposition to the use of an unfertilized clump of cells for therapeutic cloning? In an interview with Charlie Rose on PBS he defined that less–than–five–day–old cluster of cells as "an individual." Then he suggested to Dr. Harold Varmus, former director of the NIH, who was also on the program, "Why don't you experiment on me instead?" Dr. Varmus had the courtesy not to press him on that point. I would not have hesitated to ask him how that would work. Is he suffering from a disease that might be cured by therapeutic cloning? Would he be willing to have his own DNA extracted from a piece of his skin, then transferred into an unfertilized egg in order to harvest stem cells that could be used to cure him?

Senator Frist made statements that were equally puzzling to me and perhaps to thousands of others who know that, as he is the only doctor in the Senate, many of his colleagues looked to him for guidance on the issue. When we entered into a discussion on the record following my testimony on March 5, he said that he fully supported embryonic stem cell research. But after I left the room he stated that it was "irresponsible" for me to link human stem cells with therapeutic cloning, adding that he was adamantly opposed to all forms of human cloning. However, an overwhelming number of researchers and clinicians in the United States and around the world have published articles and gone on record urging therapeutic cloning to go forward. They say it might turn out to be the safest method to cure patients because it minimizes the chances of the immune system's rejection of stem cells. As a doctor Senator Frist is bound by medical ethics to prescribe the best treatment for his patients. By supporting the Brownback bill, which would not only ban therapeutic cloning but criminalize it, many disease advocates, myself included, felt that Senator Frist was making the wrong decision both as a doctor and as a senator. When it was revealed in May 2002 that he was on the short list to replace Vice President Cheney in Bush's bid for reelection, more light was shed on his opposition to therapeutic cloning.

AND THEN I TURNED FIFTY. THAT'S AN IMPORTANT MILEstone in anyone's life. Unfortunately it carried added significance for me, because I stated seven years earlier that I hoped to stand on that occasion and toast everyone who had made it possible for me to do so. I spent that evening at a festive occasion surrounded by family and friends, in good health but still seated in a wheelchair. In the weeks and months leading up to my birthday many people wanted to know what happened. Was I misinformed, naïve, or just plain ignorant when I made that statement in 1995? Some scientists offered the opinion that if the NIH had been allowed to encourage and adequately fund embryonic stem cell research immediately after those cells were first isolated in 1998 I might have made it. The cures that millions want so desperately for so many diseases might have been achieved.

I can honestly say that there is no point in becoming obsessed by what could have, should have, or might have been. My intention was to create a commotion, to provoke a reaction from scientists, politicians, and the media by proposing a difficult but not necessarily impossible challenge. I remember asking Dr. Wise Young not to give me too many details about regenerative medicine and the enormous complexities of spinal cord repair; I was willing to be the fool on the hill, even though I had promised to learn enough about the science to establish credibility. President Roosevelt, ill and disabled himself, envisioned a healthier, stronger nation and created the National Institutes of Health. Then he

challenged scientists to conquer polio, and the first vaccine was developed in less than nine years. President
Kennedy challenged the nation to land a man on the
moon in less than a decade before the technology was
even on the drawing boards. Four hundred thousand
Americans in both the public and private sector worked
together against the clock and made it possible for Neil
Armstrong to take that giant leap for mankind in 1969.
Certainly I was naïve, but I didn't see anything wrong
with emulating two of the greatest leaders of the twen-
tieth century.

All over the world there are scientists, doctors, therapists, politicians, pharmaceuticals, biotechs, foundations, universities, health care providers, and untold
others doing their utmost, even devoting their entire
lives to the relief of human suffering. What I didn't expect was that in this country, home of "Truth, Justice
and the American way," hope would be determined by
politics. When I learned that human trials for spinal
cord regeneration were delayed for two years by a small
pharmaceutical company that claimed partial ownership of a scientist's newly developed technology, I was
outraged to witness further proof that "success has a
thousand fathers, while failure is an orphan." I had always assumed that hope was based on the advance-

ment of scientific knowledge and the funding to realize its potential.

Moral and ethical questions have always attended the birth of new ideas and new technologies. Litigation of patents and the ownership of intellectual property is a more frightening obstacle. As therapies emerge and make their way into the marketplace, the pie will be very large and everyone will want a piece of it. If we don't resolve those political and economic issues soon, progress may reach an impasse, giving an inverse meaning to the concept that nothing is impossible.

Keeping hope alive requires endurance and hard work, much more than I ever anticipated. As Samuel Johnson wrote in the eighteenth century, "The excesses of hope must be expiated by pain; and expectations improperly indulged must end in disappointment." We have already experienced pain and disappointment; in fact it may continue for some time. Reaching the ultimate goals of today's biomedical research is certainly going to be extremely difficult. But ultimately I place my trust in the words of Robert F. Kennedy, who said, "The future does not belong to those who are content with today, apathetic toward common problems and their fellow man alike, timid and fearful in the face of bold projects and new ideas. Rather, it will belong to those who can blend passion, reason and courage in a personal commitment to the great enterprises and ideals of American society."

Not long ago I wrote an essay about hope. It's a story about surviving an almost impossible situation; perhaps it's also the best way I can describe how I feel about my new life:

The Lighthouse

I have always loved sailing. I loved being out on the water, in harmony with the boat, feeling the exhilaration of slicing through waves, leaving land behind. The most precious moments were shared with friends, working together to bring out the best in the boat and in ourselves.

In the late fall of 1978, I helped deliver a forty-eight-foot sloop from Connecticut to Bermuda. There were five of us onboard for the journey down the Connecticut River, eastward on Long Island Sound around the point at Montauk, then due south in search of a tiny island 564 miles off the Carolinas. We expected a passage of four to five days.

Casting off just before midnight, we caught the ebb tide that would push us quickly down-

river and out into the Sound. With a bracing 15–
knot breeze behind us, we sped past the houses
on the shoreline and watched them go dark as
people settled into their cozy beds. We had on
thermals, sweaters, and foul–weather gear to protect us against the 38–degree October night.
Clutching our mugs of coffee, ducking now and
then to avoid the stinging spray from the bow
wave, we embraced the adventure ahead.

By daybreak we had rounded Long Island
and Montauk lay astern. As it disappeared over
the horizon we knew we would not see land again
for the next four days. The wind shifted to the
west and picked up to 20 knots; the boat was "in
the groove" as we sped southward at nearly 15
miles an hour. We shifted into the routine of offshore sailing, each of us on watch for four hours
then off the next four. All of us were experienced
sailors but we hadn't met before the trip. Three
were from England, one was a Canadian friend of
the owner who lived in Toronto, and I was the
American.

The next two days passed quickly as we
enjoyed good weather, took turns preparing rea-
sonably appetizing meals, and started to get
acquainted. Although the boat was equipped with

radar and the most advanced electronic naviga-
tion system of its time, we still tracked our
progress as sailors have for centuries—with a sex-
tant and dead reckoning. Every few hours we
tuned in to the weather reports on the high-
frequency radio. On the afternoon of the third day
we didn't like what we heard.

The storm came from the north and reached
us just before dark. We were sailing directly
downwind with the mainsail and jib full out at
right angles to the boat. The rain came first, then
the following seas rose until they towered above
us. Suddenly the wind gusted to 30 and 35 knots;
all hands came on deck to take down the jib and
put two reefs in the main. Even with the reduced
sail area, we were now sledding down mountain-
ous waves, the bow crashing into the troughs
below as the storm turned into a full-blown gale.

We couldn't see anything beyond the dim
glow of the running lights. Adrenaline rushed
through our veins as we fought to stay in control
of the situation. I was afraid that the electronic
systems might fail if water flooded the cockpit
and found its way below, making it impossible to
determine our position. We weren't maintaining a
course; we were just trying to survive.

The gale pursued us through the night and into the following day. When we came off watch we stumbled below, grabbed a few crackers to keep something in our stomachs, and crawled into our bunks. The only relief was that with the dawn we were able to see the chaos around us. Even though the helmsman's compass was swinging wildly back and forth, now we knew that our average heading was south. And then we saw the light.

It was dim and distant; we could only see it when the boat was lifted on the crest of a wave. Every time we came up, all eyes strained to find it again through the blinding rain. Soon we realized that the light flashed for two seconds at ten-second intervals. Someone went below to check the charts. Dead ahead of us, forty miles away, was Gibb's Hill Lighthouse at Southampton, Bermuda.

Lighthouses—tall, sturdy, and built to withstand the pounding surf and raging winds—warn passing ships to avoid crashing into rocks or dangerous reefs near shore. Lighthouses have guided sailors through troubled waters for as long as anyone can remember. Seeing that lighthouse was like being held in the arms of a parent or a long-lost friend. Now it didn't matter if our modern equipment failed. All we had to do was not lose sight of it and let nothing keep us from reaching its warm embrace.

At some time, often when we least expect it, we all have to face overwhelming challenges. We are more troubled than we have ever been before; we may doubt that we have what it takes to endure. It is very tempting to give up, yet we have to find the will to keep going. But even when we discover what motivates us, we realize that we can't go the distance alone.

When the unthinkable happens, the lighthouse is hope. Once we find it, we must cling to it with absolute determination, much as our crew did when we saw the light of Gibb's Hill that October afternoon. Hope must be as real, and built on the same solid foundation, as a lighthouse; in that way it is different from optimism or wishful thinking. When we have hope, we discover powers within ourselves we may have never known— the power to make sacrifices, to endure, to heal, and to love. Once we choose hope, everything is possible. We are all on this sea together. But the lighthouse is always there, ready to show us the way home.

Postscript

This is the evening of May 27, 2003, the eighth anniversary of the accident. That I call it "the accident" is perhaps an indication that I still don't blame myself or my horse or a conspiracy of the Fates for what happened. Given all the inexplicable acts of violence, injustice and cruelty, mixed with the unexpected small miracles of kindness and happiness that we see in the world every day, I remain convinced that life is chaos, but that it is within our power to establish order and meaning.

Today I received many phone calls and emails from friends and family checking in to see how I'm doing. Most of them wanted to make sure that I had a plan for the day, enough activities to keep me from sinking into depression. For the first time I sensed that others were more reflective and saddened by the memory than I was.

It's Tuesday, a workday much like any other. It started at eight with sending Wilf off to school, followed by coffee, cereal, then three hours of physical therapy and preparation for the day. Chris Fantini, the aide on duty this morning, began by working my arms and legs through a passive range of motion, repeating the pattern that was first established in rehabilitatin during the summer of 1995. After a long night lying immobile, my legs elevated to reduce swelling and my arms strapped in splints to keep them straight, it felt good to have my knees bent and pushed towards my chest and my arms stretched backwards behind my head. I enjoyed the tingling sensation as blood flowed again into my hands and feet, and welcomed the pounding of fists on my chest and back as Chris and my nurse Dolly Arro worked to loosen fluid that had accumulated in my lungs while I slept. Then they placed electrodes on my shoulders and arms and attached the wires from the E-stim machine. Both pulled up chairs on opposite sides of the bed to support me as the electrical stimulation worked to exercise and maintain the muscle mass of my deltoids, biceps and triceps. Tomorrow we'll give the upper body a rest and work my legs. Finally the bandages that hold the ventilator tubing in place in my throat were changed, Chris and Dolly rolled me from side to side as they dressed me in the clothes I'd picked for today, and by noon I was positioned in my chair and headed for the office.

Normally my assistant Laurie Hawkins would bring up the mail and the list of phone calls to be returned. Today we dispensed with the normal routine because I had a 12.30 meeting with the Israeli ambassador to the U.S. and two representatives from the Consulate. The agenda was to discuss the details of an invitation to visit Israel at the end of July. I explained that I was most interested in going to hospitals and rehab centers to meet victims of violence, especially children and patients with spinal cord injuries. We agreed to spend most of the time in Tel Aviv, with side trips first to Jerusalem then Haifa, to visit Dr. Michal Schwarz and her colleagues at the Weizmann Institute of Science. In response to my concerns about security, the ambassador advised me not to use public transportation or go to a discotheque at 2 A.M. Not a problem. When the Israeli delegation left, I reflected that it was my present condition that had brought about this truly unique opportunity.

By 2:30, I had caught up with some office work, eaten lunch and was in the middle of a magazine interview about celebrities and public service. As I launched into my oft-repeated thesis that celebrities have the right to address issues (as long as they know what they're talking about), I looked up at the clock and noticed it was exactly 3:01. I hadn't been watching the clock all day, and I have no idea what made me look just then. But that was the moment: at 3:01 P.M. eight years ago I galloped out of the starting box at the cross-country jumping course in Culpepper, Virginia. At 3:02 I was on the ground with a broken neck and an injured spinal cord.

As I carried on the conversation with the reporter, I watched the second hand crawl in slow motion. I saw myself in my customary light blue t-shirt, the blue chest protector with the yellow stripe, my stirrups hiked up, the riding crop in my right hand. I felt the oppressive humidity, little rivers of sweat running down my forehead, remembered wishing I had taken a few more gulps of water before the start.

Then it was over. I'm sure the writer on the other end of the phone had no idea that a part of me had briefly gone away. Emotion didn't overcome me, nor did I have to try to suppress it, nor was I distracted by an external event such as Matthew's graduation from college which took place on May 27 last year. What was different today, on this anniversary, was a new perspective. I wasn't drawn into an internal debate about what might have been done differently, which used to provoke guilt and regret. This year I observed and partially re–lived a defining moment in my life, but remained engaged in the present and making plans for the future. This year I learned acceptance.

THE JOURNEY TOWARDS ACCEPTANCE AND THE DISCOVERY that we can find meaning and purpose in the face of chaos and adversity has been intensely personal. The outside world remains as challenging and often frustrating as ever.

The most consistent source of frustration is still politics. A year after writing the chapter entitled "Hope", the U.S. still has no federal policy on stem cells. Fortunately the bill that would ban somatic cell nuclear transfer has not reached the Senate floor for a vote, but neither has the bill that would permit it. As a result, the U.K., Sweden, Israel and Singapore are still in the lead. Many of our best scientists have either left or are threatening to defect. Young post–docs who would like to work with stem cells are choosing other fields because they need to pay back student loans. In spite of major breakthroughs in stem cell research, President Bush refuses to approve federal funding for the creation of new stem cell lines that scientists urgently need.

In fact, urgency is the heart of the matter for scientists and patient advocates alike. Some researchers are eager to go forward with human trials in the near future but find their hands tied by public policy. Others seem afraid to make the leap from the bench to the bedside; it is one thing to make a mistake with a mouse and quite another to cause harm to a human being. At the same time, I and the vast majority of patients I know are increasingly willing to accept reasonable risks. When a scientist tells me that a botched experiment might set the field back ten years, I think of the achievements of Jonas Salk. Not only did he develop a vaccine for influenza in time to save the lives of thousands of soldiers during World War II, but he is also credited with the first vaccine to prevent polio. He took risks by working quickly; some contend he may have plagiarized his colleagues, but if he did so I maintain it was in service to humanity.

The Christopher Reeve Paralysis Foundation is rooted in the belief that there is nothing more important than relieving human suffering, and we fully understand there may be setbacks and casualties along the way. With that in mind, the CRPF and the Coalition for the Advancement of Medical Research, representing more than eighty disease groups, universities and scientists, have worked hard in the last year to maintain a sense of urgency and circumvent the obstacles to progress. Because the federal government has failed to act, we have become advocates for initiatives in the states. The first success was achieved in California, which passed legislation in September 2002 that allows scientists there to perform research using stem cells derived from any source. Today New Jersey, New York, Illinois, Kentucky, Virginia, Maryland, Rhode Island, Tennessee, Massachusetts and Washington are all considering legislation that mirrors the current law in California.

Recently, we have taken other aggressive steps to promote translational research. Our foundation has set aside more than $5 million to award a scientist or institution that is prepared for human trials. The New York State Spinal Cord Injury Research Trust has set aside $15 million for the creation of a Center of Research Excellence with the proviso that human trials will begin within 3–5 years. Earlier this month, the Christopher Reeve Paralysis Act of 2003 was introduced simultaneously in both the U.S. Senate and House of Representatives. It provides federal funding for research leading to a cure for paralysis, research into proactive therapies to improve patient outcomes, and quality of life issues for people living with paralysis. The bill would benefit all who suffer from strokes, multiple sclerosis, brain injury, ALS and other causes in addition to spinal cord injury – nearly 3 million Americans.

PEOPLE OFTEN ASK WHAT KEEPS ME GOING AND HOW I maintain such a positive attitude. Certainly the privilege of being a public figure who can interact with scientists, politicians and the media on behalf of those whose voices will never be heard is an important factor. I am also driven by my core belief that nothing is impossible. But the truth is that eight years post–injury, I feel that I am engaged in a constant struggle. I'm not always positive, nor do I feel that I'm marching steadily forward; it's more like two steps forward, one step back. I make progress with exercise – on the FES bicycle, or in the pool where I can extend my arms or push off from the wall like a swimmer starting the backstroke. Gradually I become stronger and signals from my brain make their way down my spinal cord, past the site of injury, faster and faster until my legs respond the instant I say "Go". Then I get an infection from whatever bacteria haven't been killed by the chlorine, I'm back on antibiotics and can't go to the pool for six weeks. When I return I have to start over.

In February I was the subject of an "investigational procedure" designed to free me from the ventilator.

Doctors in Cleveland, Ohio, led by Anthony DiMarco and Raymond Onders, surgically implanted electrodes in both the left and right diaphragms, with wires running to an exit site on the left side of my chest. When a specially designed transmitter is activated the electrodes fire simultaneously, the diaphragms move and generate normal breathing. At first the diaphragms are weak after years of disuse and it's extremely difficult to endure even five to ten minutes of so-called "diaphragm pacing" without becoming desperate for more air. But gradually the diaphragms start to recover from atrophy and it becomes easier to "pace" for increasing periods of time.

By mid-April I was pacing as much as five hours a day. Then, for no apparent reason, I stopped dead in my tracks. I couldn't pace at all; within a minute after activating the transmitter I was gasping like a fish out of water and had to be put back on the ventilator. A CT-scan proved that nearly a pint of fluid had accumulated in the plural cavity between my left lung and diaphragm, restricting any movement. A cardiothoracic sugeon had to insert a long tube through my ribcage in the back and suction the fluid out. I tried to lighten the mood by commenting that it looked like a strawberry daiquiri, but no one laughed. Once again I had to start over.

Now I'm used to these setbacks and accept them as the price I have to pay for becoming ever more aggressive about my situation over the years. Whether I'm arguing public policy, pushing for more funding, questioning scientists, or challenging my body to function, I know that a graph of my progress will look like a week on the stock market rather than the straight line I once imagined.

Along this journey there are constant adventures and misadventures. But where there is pain, there is also genuine joy. Our house is often filled with laughter. My family and all the dedicated people who work with us take pleasure at every opportunity, no matter how small or absurd. Recently I was pacing, carrying on a conversation with Dana, and trying to eat salad at the same time. The trick is to chew on the inhale and swallow on the exhale. I mistimed it, and a good-sized piece of lettuce went down the wrong way. I was choking and laughing at the same time as Dolly went to work to suction the offending vegetable out of my windpipe. After a few minutes it came up, my face turned from blue back to pink again, and another instance of chaos was put behind us. Perhaps that sums up my life now in a nutshell.

The rest of today was pretty routine. At 4:30 I joined Mitch Stoller, President and CEO of our foundation, on a conference call with a gentleman suffering from spinal meningitis who is interested in supporting our work with a very generous donation. I paced for more than six hours as I dictated this postscript to my daughter Alexandra, who stopped by for a couple of days on the way to her summer job in New Haven. Dana picked up Will from school, gave him a quick snack, and then they went off to hockey practice. Matthew just returned to England after some filming with me for the next installment of the three–part documentary he's making about my progress.

Just a few moments ago we stopped for dinner and tuned in the evening news. Apparently scientists have isolated a master cell that can be extracted from fertilized embryos without causing any damage. Embryonic stem cells can be derived from the master cell, which will enable scientists to create an unlimited number of cell lines in an absolutely uncontroversial procedure. If this report is accurate, an enormous breakthrough has been achieved that will revolutionize the entire field of stem cell research. I'm going to look into it first thing tomorrow.

Still Me

Christopher Reeve

The whole world held its breath when Christopher Reeve struggled for life on Memorial Day, 1995. Thrown headfirst from his horse, the screen idol adored by millions – the critically acclaimed actor, the man who was Superman – was left incapable of movement.

Yet despite his paralysis, the man who cannot move has not stopped moving. He has testified before Congress, made his directorial debut and written *Still Me*, the moving, wise, passionate and gripping story of his life.

'Brave, funny and deeply moving'
Sunday Telegraph

'Fascinating and utterly lacking in self-pity'
Guardian

'A simply told tale of a generous soul'
Mail on Sunday

Arrow Books
£6.99
0099257289

The Lent Jewels

David Hughes

In one spring month of 1856 Archibald Campbell Tait (later to be Archbishop of Canterbury) and his wife Catharine suffered the loss of five daughters, aged between two and ten, in an epidemic of scarlet fever. In his diary Tait refers to these beloved children as 'the lent jewels'.

The couple bore their bereavement with a fortitude that could be sustained only by faith. Without similar convictions, but in the hope of laying bare a comparable belief for himself, David Hughes explores the themes of love and loss, intermingling his own experience, both as child and father, with the story of another of Tait's contemporaries, someone with a different but nonetheless powerful focus on life, a man known only as 'Walter', author of the erotic memoir *My Secret Life*. At the same time Catharine was drowning her grief in words by writing a heartbreaking account of her children's deaths. All these presences, and more modern ones, haunt the chapters of this many-layered documentary.

With a dexterity of style and abundance of sympathy that have made him so appealing a writer, Hughes delves into two centuries of underlying attitudes to sex, dreams and mortality, in an effort to reconcile them in his own daily life. The result of his sometimes sad but always eager search is splendidly uplifting.

Arrow Books
£6.99
0099435071

J. K. Rowling

Sean Smith

J.K. Rowling is a household name. Creator of the most famous and best-loved character in contemporary fiction, she is also the author of her own escape from a depressing existence on the verge of destitution. The tale of the quiet woman writing away at a café table, making a solitary cup of tea and a glass of water last for hours while her baby daughter slept in her pram may have become a cliché, but it has also served as an inspiration for millions.

Sean Smith's compelling biography presents J. K. Rowling, the multi-millionaire author whose books have taken the world by storm. Alongside that, there is the story of Joanne Rowling, a dreamy, rather shy woman whose brilliance in translating her dreams into prose changed her life. Fully updated, this edition tells the story of her phenomenal rise to fame and fortune.

'Why bother with a biography? Surely we know her story well enough by now? That's what I thought until I opened Sean Smith's captivating tale. By the time I finished the first chapter, I had entered a world so very, very different from Harry Potter yet with such strong links to it, that I was forced to read the book in one sitting . . . What makes this book outstanding is how Smith has tracked down the sources of JK's inspiration.'

Daily Express

Arrow Books
£6.99
0099445425

The Flamboya Tree

Clara Olink Kelly

"Why didn't you try to escape?' That was all she said. I had imagined my grandmother telling us how lovely it was to see us at last. I saw again in my mind's eye the barbwire fences and the soldiers with the glistening bayonets, and felt once more that excruciating fear in the pit of my stomach. Try to escape? Lots of people had tried to escape."

When the Japanese invaded the beautiful Indonesian island of Java during the Second World War, Clara Kelly was four years old. Her family was separated, her father sent to work on the Burma railway, and she was sent to a 'women's camp', together with her mother and her two brothers, one a six-week-old baby. They were interned there until the end of the war.

Clara's descriptions of the appalling deprivations and impersonal brutality of the camp – standing in the baking heat for hours of 'Tenko' roll-call, living on one cup of rice a day – are countered by the courage and resilience shown by all the internees, most poignantly her own mother.

Arrow Books
£6.99
0099445530

BUY *Arrow*

Order further *Arrow* titles from your local bookshop,
or have them delivered direct to your door by
Bookpost

☐ *Still Me*	0099257289	£6.99
☐ *The Lent Jewels*	0099435071	£6.99
☐ *J. K. Rowling*	0099445425	£6.99
☐ *The Flamboya Tree*	0099445530	£6.99
☐ *The Little Book of Life's Wisdom*	0099415798	£2.99

FREE POST AND PACKING
Overseas customers allow £2.00 per paperback

By PHONE: 01624 677237

By POST: Random House Books
C/o Bookpost, PO Box 29, Douglas
Isle of Man, IM99 1BQ

By FAX: 01624 670923

By EMAIL: bookshop@enterprise.net

Cheques (payable to Bookpost) and credit cards
accepted

Prices and availability subject to change without notice.
Allow 28 days for delivery.

When placing your order, please mention if you do not wish to
receive any additional information.

www.randomhouse.co.uk